Dedication

To all women who desire to improve their quality of life, while being encouraged along the way.

Acknowledgments

Thank you, Holy Spirit, for giving me creative ideas to assist women throughout the land.

Introduction

Pearls of Wisdom Quotes & Journal Volume I contains 90 thought-provoking, inspirational quotes (a 3-month supply) for women that will spark change and growth. After each quote, there is an explanation to provide insight into the quote. Many of the explanations include a biblical reference, and the Bible version is denoted in the parenthetical marking preceding or following each scripture. After each explanation is a set of blank lines to be used for your personal reflection. As you read the quote and the corresponding explanation, allow your inner woman to speak out to you concerning your innermost feelings. Write them down. This journal is to share your thoughts, desires, and feelings with yourself. No one is going to see your writing unless you opt to share.

Therefore, take a moment each day to write your truth. Writing is liberating and can assist in alleviating stress. You would be doing yourself a

PEARLS of Wisdom
Quotes & Journal

Volume I

Dr. C.

www.clfpublishing.org
909.315.3161

Copyright © 2022 by Cassundra White-Elliott.

All rights reserved. No portion of this book may be reproduced, stored in a retrieval system, or transmitted by any form or any means electronically, photocopied, recorded, or any other except for brief quotations in printed reviews, without the prior permission of the publisher.

Cover design by Senir Design. Contact info: info@senirdesign.com

ISBN #978-1-945102-91-2

Printed in the United States of America.

special favor by searching inside yourself to bring deep-rooted anxieties and desires to the surface. Do not suppress them, as doing so can lead to overwhelming stress, fear, and possibly depression. This journal can be used as a method of release as well as a tool for recording what God reveals to you *about* you and your life. Keep it close by. Maybe carry it with you in your handbag, car, or briefcase. Once you have completed Volume I and ended the first quarter of the year, remember to get the next volume for the next quarter.

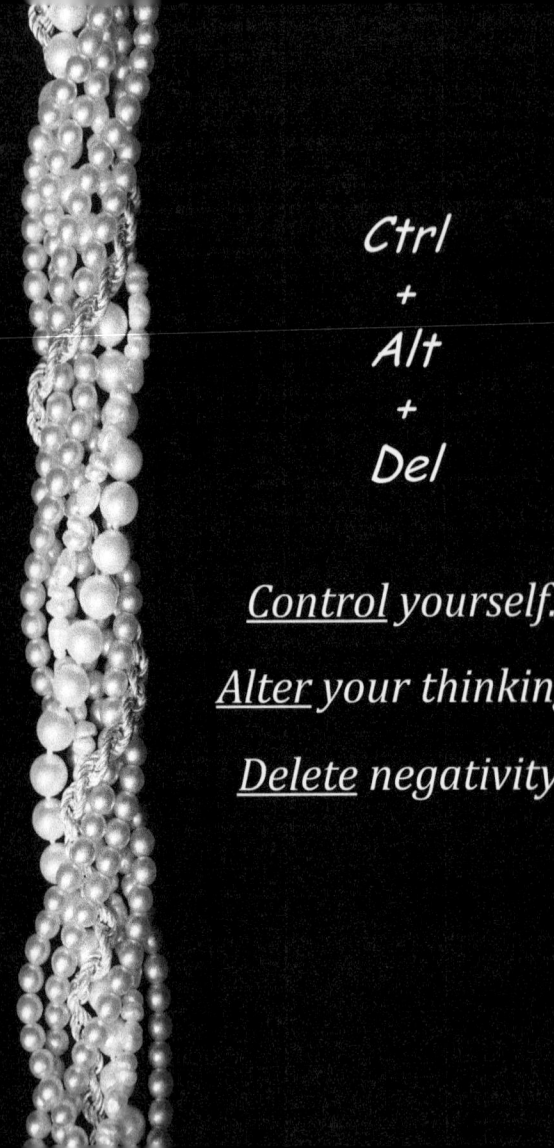

Similar to selecting keyboard controls to obtain the best outcome when performing a task, *control* your life by choosing the most useful actions, avoiding those that will cause destruction. Why waste time trying to control other people, what they do or how they think? All you can do is *control* yourself. Stop trying to *control* situations by controlling other people. *Control* yourself by *altering* your thinking. Proverbs 23:7 says, *"As a man thinketh in his heart, so is he."* What you spend time meditating on will eventually manifest in your life. If you focus on positivity, you will produce positive results from the efforts you expend. On the other hand, if you consistently cultivate negativity in your thoughts, your words, and your deeds, you will breed negative results. *Delete* negativity from your life today. Doing so will lead to a healthier lifestyle.

Reflection

_____

_____

_____

_____

_____

_____

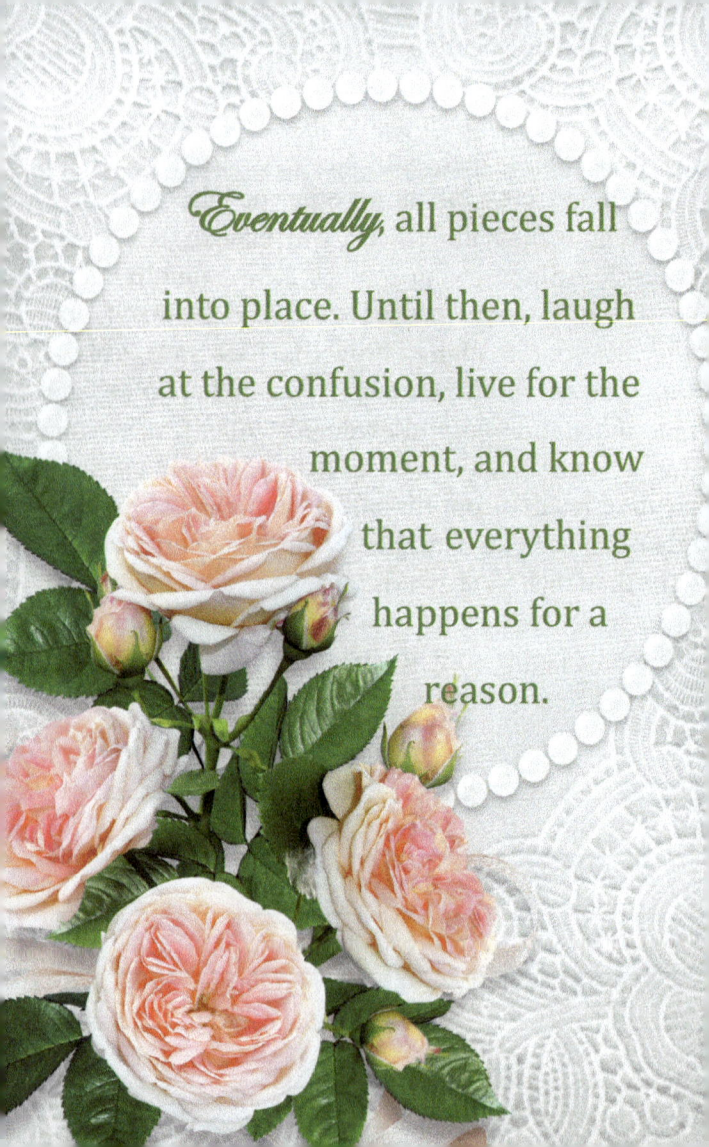

Eventually, all pieces fall into place. Until then, laugh at the confusion, live for the moment, and know that everything happens for a reason.

Romans 8:28 says, *"And we know that all things work together for good to those who love God, to those who are the called according to His purpose"* (NKJV). Although we may not understand why things happen, we know who is controlling the universe. All power rests in His hands. So, if we trust Him, we understand everything will work out in the end. Until then, breathe. Relax. Hold on to your peace. And, by all means, keep your eyes and head uplifted toward the hills, knowing your help comes from the Lord (Psalm 121:1-2), for He is the Almighty, omniscient, omnipotent, and omnipresent God. He is the divine creator, and He will make every crooked path straight. Place all of your faith and trust in Him. He will not fail you.

Reflection

_____

_____

_____

_____

_____

_____

_____

What is the purpose of beholding godly wisdom but refraining from utilizing it? We are told in James 1:5, *"If any of you lacks wisdom, you should ask God, who gives generously to all without finding fault, and it will be given to you"* (NIV). The Lord has everything we need, including wisdom to navigate through this world system. So, if God grants us the wisdom we need, thereby giving us the key to the path we should take in life, we should follow through. That takes a walk of integrity, doing what we know is right regardless if it is difficult or unattractive. In the end, God will be pleased by our actions, and we will reap the benefits of a life of integrity.

Reflection

_____

_____

_____

_____

_____

_____

_____

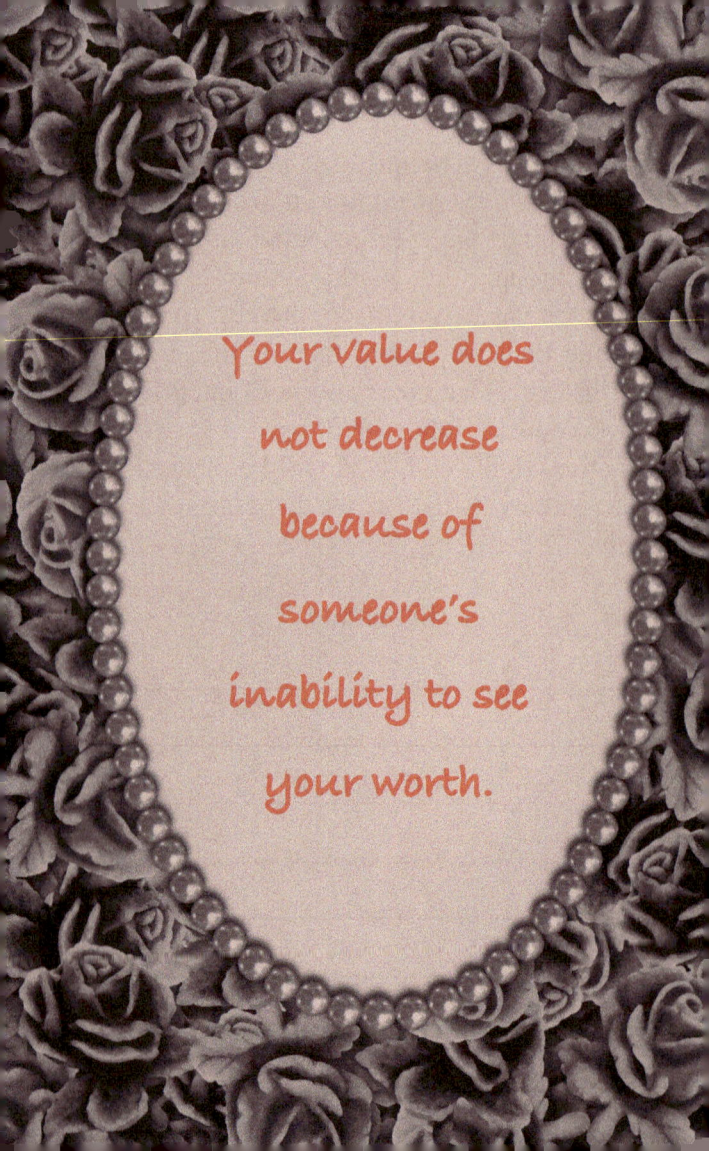

Experiences, age, culture, education, and religious beliefs all impact what a person considers valuable. A person's daily decisions, whether conscious or unconscious, includes determining the value of others as it relates to his/her own life. People decide whether or not other people will add value to their life. This is shown in their response and/or attention given to other people. When one person values another, he/she listens to what the other has to say as he/she shares thoughts and ideas. When a person is devalued, his/her perspectives and ideas are disregarded as worthless. Whether or not someone deems you to be valuable or not does not diminish the actual value you possess. God created each of us as a rare gem. Some people will cherish you and see your worth, and others will not. Either way, regardless of their perception, your actual worth remains intact.

Reflection

_____

_____

_____

_____

_____

Stay committed to your decisions, but remain flexible in your approach.

Tony Robbins

Habakkuk 2:2 says, *"The LORD answered me: Write down this vision; clearly inscribe it on tablets so one may easily read it"* (CSB). When God gives you a vision (a plan) for your life, commit to carrying it out to bring the plan to fruition. However, you can prevent headaches and heartaches by being flexible in your approach. There may be more than one approach to achieving your goal. Be open to trying an alternate method that will allow you to achieve the desired end. Have multiple plans in place, so if Plan A does not pan out successfully, move on to Plan B.

Reflection

_____

_____

_____

_____

_____

_____

_____

_____

Always be yourself and have faith in yourself. Do not go out and find a successful personality and try to duplicate it.

Bruce Lee

Psalm 139:24 informs us of the unique design God employed to fashion us along with how we should respond to Him as a result: *"I praise you because I am fearfully and wonderfully made; your works are wonderful, I know that full well."* We should praise the Lord everyday for making us unique and special in His sight. There is no other person who is exactly like us. We may share similarities with other people, but no one shares the exact same set of traits as we do. First off, God made us in His image. Then, He added a little spice, a little pizzazz, and a little flair into each one of us, thereby causing an individual pattern and result to manifest. Enjoy your unique design, and praise God while being the beautiful person He created.

Reflection

_____

_____

_____

_____

_____

_____

_____

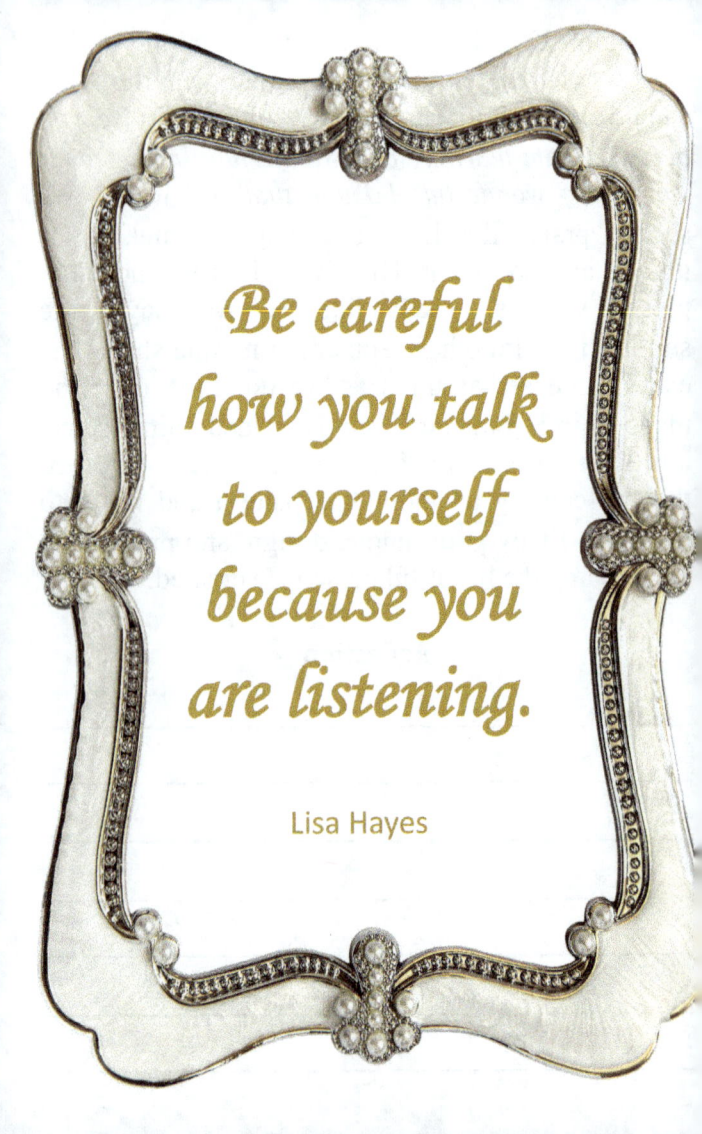

As a child, you heard many words from your parents, teachers, family members, friends, and even strangers. Those words helped to shape the person you became by either helping to build a strong moral character and mental fortitude within you or causing low self-esteem to develop and/or reckless behavior to manifest. As an adult, you are the main person to speak into your life. Therefore, you must be careful what you say because your ears are ever present, internalizing it all. Remember, life and death are in the power of the tongue; speak life (Proverbs 18:21). And, speak those things that be not as though they were (Romans 4:17). When you speak about yourself or about plans you have, be positive, loving, and kind. Refrain from speaking negatively, and do not allow others to speak negatively about you or your life either.

Reflection

_____

_____

_____

_____

_____

_____

Sacrifice LIKE *Esther*

Love LIKE *Ruth*

Serve LIKE *Martha*

Pray LIKE *Hannah*

Believe LIKE *Mary*

Dance LIKE *Miriam*

If you look around yourself, you can point to women who have been instrumental in your life, serving as examples in one area or another. There are women who taught you various lessons in your life that have been instrumental in shaping the woman you are today. In the Word of God, there are other women you can glean from, such as Esther, who was willing to sacrifice herself for her people the Jews. Another is Ruth, who showed love to her mother-in-law. Martha, who was very hospitable to the Lord and others, is another good example. Hannah is an example of a prayer warrior who prayed until her dream was manifested. Mary exhibited strong faith in God, and Miriam danced as she praised the Lord. Remember, just as you had wonderful, strong women to shape and direct your life, you can assist in shaping another woman's life. She is waiting for you.

Reflection

_____

_____

_____

_____

_____

"Be strong and courageous. Do not be afraid; do not be discouraged, for the LORD your God will be with you wherever you go."

Joshua 1:9b (NIV)

When you are striving towards a goal, there is a chance that your efforts may not prove successful just as there is the possibility that your efforts will bring about the desired results. Despite the outcome of your efforts, never give up no matter the circumstances. Be strong in the face of adversity. Be courageous to keep focused on your goal. You are a champion, and you will overcome the dreaded obstacles. Champions take failure as a learning opportunity, so take in all you can and run with it. Be the best you can be and do not ever give up on your dreams. If your dreams are worth dreaming, they should be worth the effort it takes to bring them to reality. Do not allow fear to deter you from your goals.

Reflection

_____

_____

_____

_____

_____

_____

_____

Wake up with determination.

Go to bed with satisfaction.

Every night, make a point to compose a to-do list before retiring to bed. Your list should consist of manageable tasks that can be completed in the duration of the next calendar day. When composing your to-do list, consider your work schedule and other chores and tasks that take precedence. Do not endeavor to add items to the list that cannot be completed in the available hours. When composing the list, also schedule the exact time you can and will complete the task. Using times frames will greatly increase the possibility of the task being completed. For example, if you work an eight-hour day and some of the items on your list include making phone calls, consider making the calls during your breaks or your lunch hour rather than waiting until you are off work. If you wake up each day with a list of tasks you are determined to complete and actually complete them, you will go to bed satisfied.

Reflection

_____

_____

_____

_____

_____

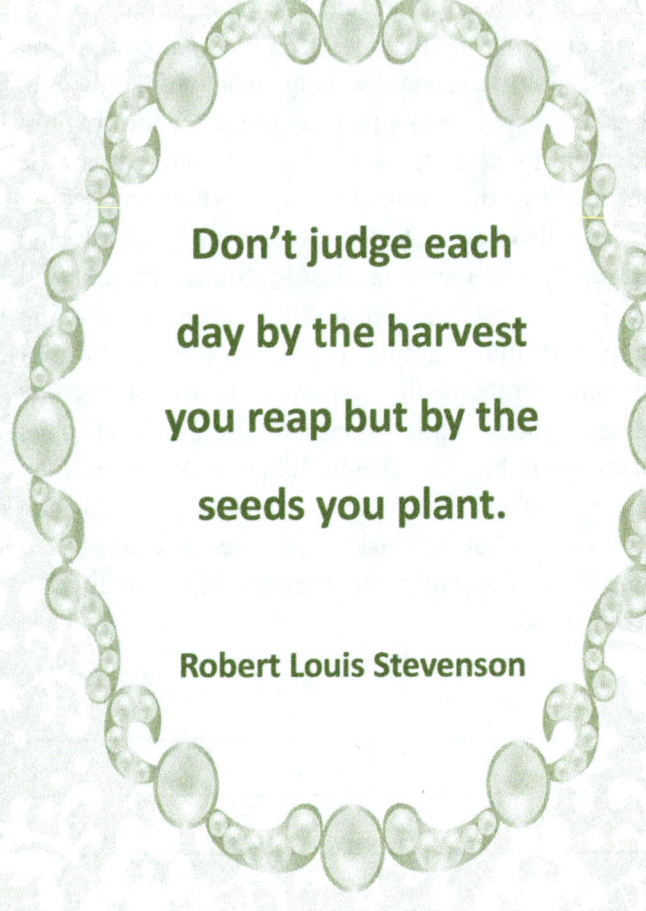

Acts 20:35 says, *"In everything I did, I showed you that by this kind of hard work we must help the weak, remembering the words the Lord Jesus himself said: 'It is more blessed to give than to receive.'"* Jesus is a great example of how to be a giver. He never concerned Himself with what others did for Him. He was concerned about how He could sow into their lives. Likewise, we should plant as many seeds as we can into other people's lives and into the Kingdom of God. As God gives to us, we should give to others. God will return unto us a harvest in due season.

Reflection

_____

_____

_____

_____

_____

_____

_____

_____

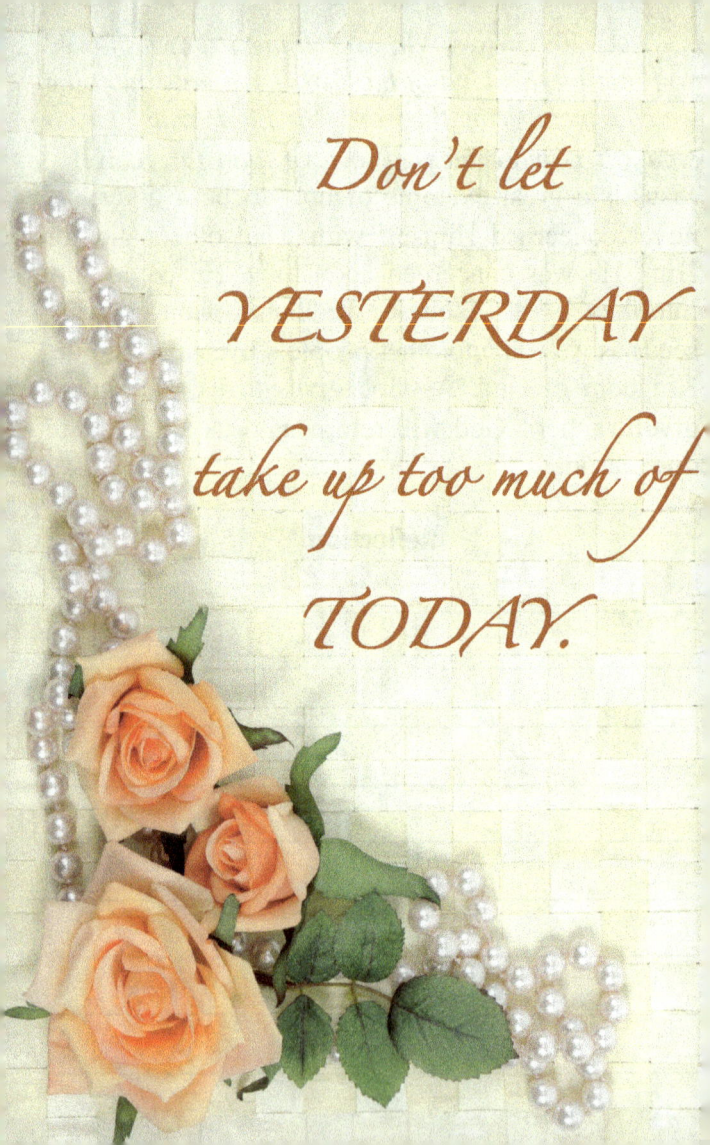

Apostle Paul in Philippians 3:13-14 tells us, *"Brethren, I count not myself to have apprehended: but this one thing I do, forgetting those things which are behind, and reaching forth unto those things which are before, I press toward the mark for the prize of the high calling of God in Christ Jesus."* This verse tells us to not allow the circumstances, choices, and occurrences of yesterday to sit too heavily on our minds that we cannot focus on moving forward. The past has a way of creeping into our memory and debilitating our progress. That is a trick of the enemy. Control the thoughts of your mind and decide what you will focus on and give attention. Keep your mind free from regrets about things you cannot change. Stay focused on creating a brighter today and a more prosperous future.

Reflection

_____

_____

_____

_____

_____

_____

Do you realize your life is a stage play and every new season in your life is a different scene or a different act in the play? It's true. The world is a stage, and on it, we perform. Each day is a new opportunity for a new adventure in this thing called life. Take advantage of each opportunity to add revelation to your story. Make sure each day, each scene, each act makes an impact and adds substance to your story. Afterall, someone is reading and/or watching the story of your life right now.

Reflection

_____

_____

_____

_____

_____

_____

_____

_____

_____

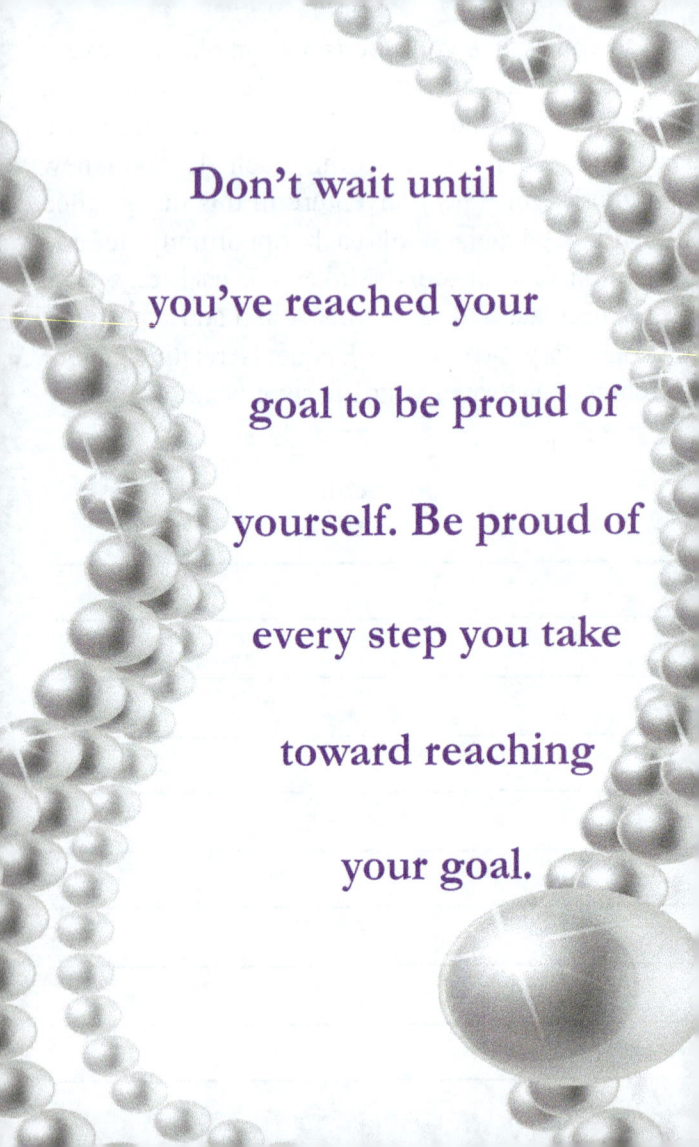

Don't wait until you've reached your goal to be proud of yourself. Be proud of every step you take toward reaching your goal.

Most goals, whether short-term or long-term, are achieved by navigating through a series of steps. Each step in the overall process can be considered a small victory or achievement in manifesting the overall goal. Celebrate each victory for it is a milestone in your overall plan! Celebrating will do wonders for your self-esteem and keep you motivated to achieve the end goal.

Reflection

_____
_____
_____
_____
_____
_____
_____
_____
_____
_____
_____
_____

When fear wants to creep in and overwhelm you, allow your tenacity to rise to the surface. When circumstances arise and your resolve seems to want to dissipate, and you suddenly feel weak and faint, allow your inner strength to rise to the surface. Galatians 6:9 (KJV), *"And let us not be weary in well doing: for in due season we shall reap, if we faint not."* When you do not know what to do and your human nature tells you to think and figure it out by coming up with a viable solution, take the following advice from the Word of God instead: *"Trust in the LORD with all thine heart; and lean not unto thine own understanding. In all thy ways acknowledge him, and he shall direct thy paths"* (Proverbs 3:5-6). The truth of the Word of God will offer us strength and wisdom. Accept the gifts, and use them in your times of trouble.

Reflection

_____

_____

_____

_____

_____

_____

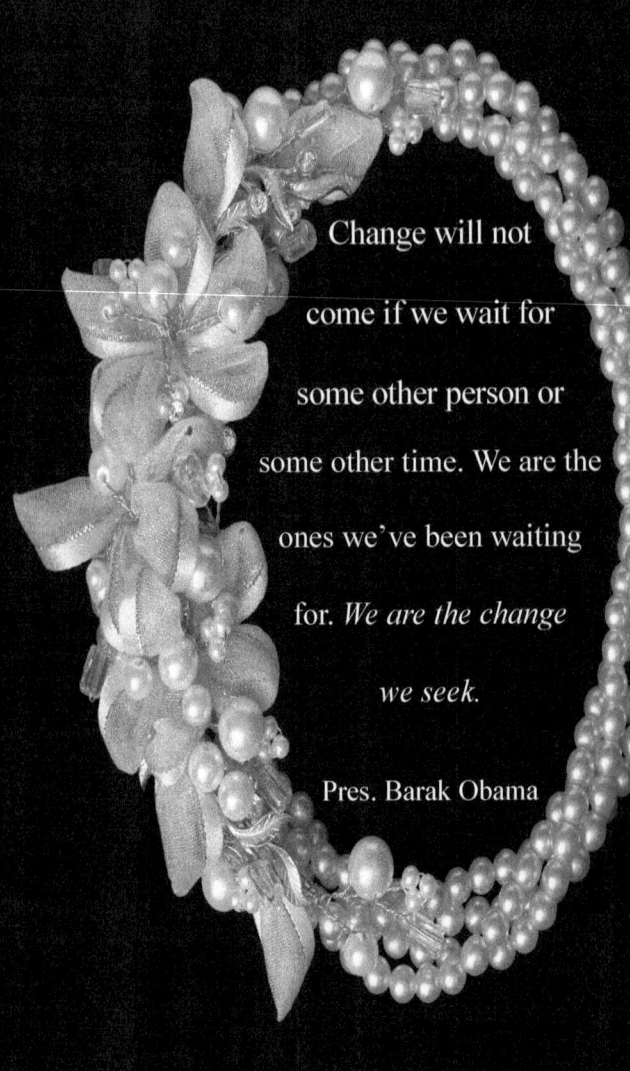

Only changemakers can effectuate change. Ask yourself, "Have I resolved to maintaining the status quo, or do I desire change in my circumstances, in my community, and in the world at large?" If you answered you desire change, I implore you to take a step in the right direction toward that change today. You do not have to be wealthy, educated, a keynote speaker, or a Rhode scholar. All you have to do is use the power within your voice, and your voice will be heard. If you dare to open your mouth, someone will dare to listen.

Reflection

_____

_____

_____

_____

_____

_____

_____

_____

_____

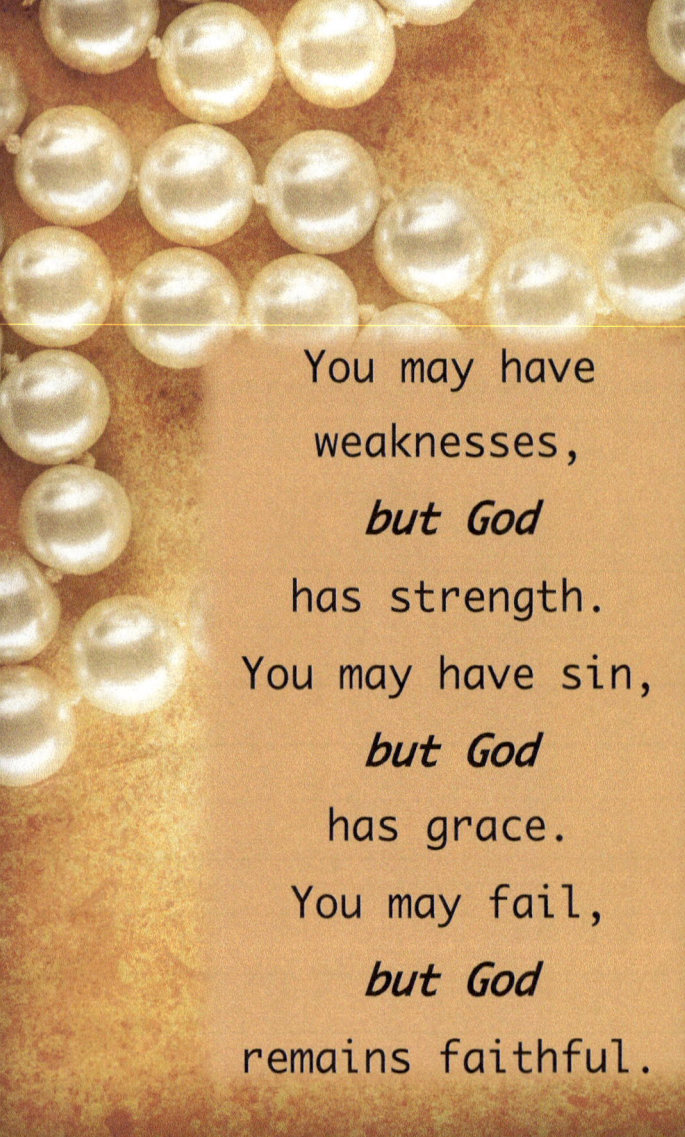

Oftentimes, we attempt to operate our lives using our own human strength, rather than appealing to the wisdom, strength, and grace of God. God is merciful, and He is a god of grace. Through each and every situation we may find ourselves facing, God has everything we have need to get through it. *"But we have this treasure in earthen vessels, that the excellency of the power may be of God, and not of us. We are troubled on every side, yet not distressed; we are perplexed, but not in despair; Persecuted, but not forsaken; cast down, but not destroyed; Always bearing about in the body the dying of the Lord Jesus, that the life also of Jesus might be made manifest in our body"* II Cor. 4:7-12. By design, God chose weak and feeble humans to operate through in order that all who witnessed His miracle working power would know it was not done by human power but by His own.

Reflection

_____

_____

_____

_____

_____

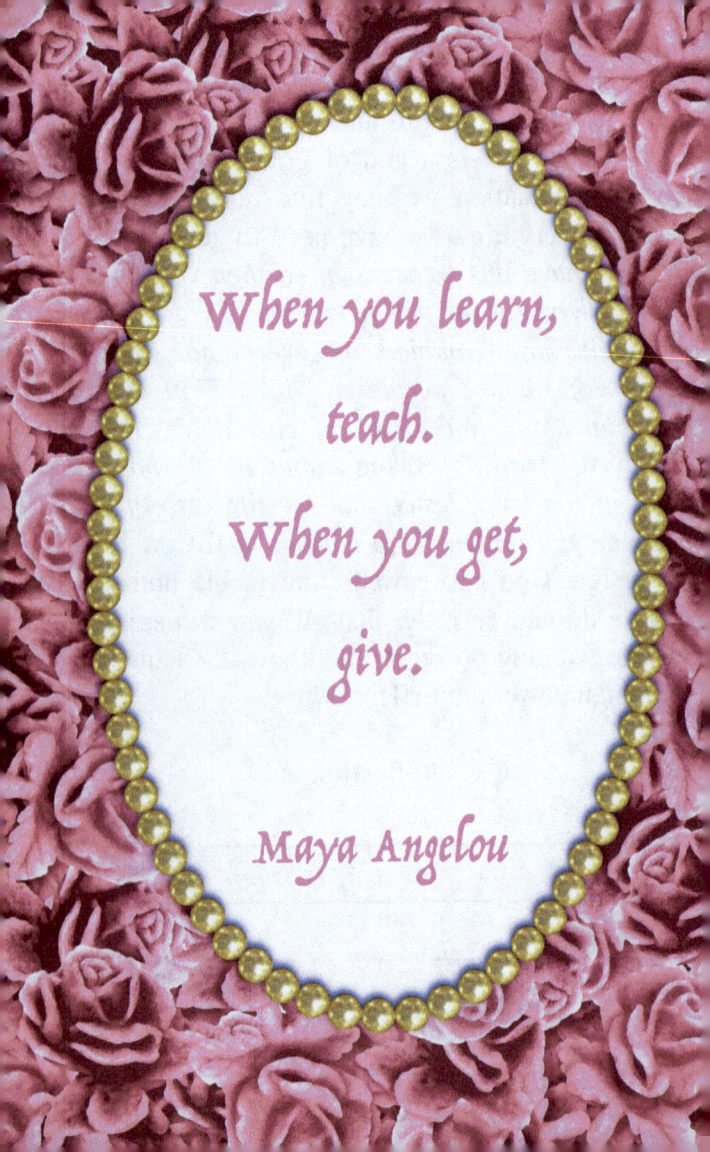

The Lord has poured a wealth of knowledge into you, whether it is knowledge from your experiences, your education, your joys, or your pains. The knowledge is not for you to keep to yourself, so your belly can be full. No, the knowledge you have is for you to share with others. Teach someone what you know, show them they way. Furthermore, when you receive from the Lord, whether it is finances, information, clothing, food, or whatever God blesses you with, you must freely give out as God freely gave to you.

Reflection

_____

_____

_____

_____

_____

_____

_____

_____

_____

Be the kind of woman that when your feet touch the floor each morning, the devil says, "Oh, crap! She's up!"

Acts 19:15 records: *"And the evil spirit answered and said, Jesus I know, and Paul I know; but who are ye?"* Does the enemy know who you are? Are you actively involved in the building of God's Kingdom to the point that the devil knows your name, your works, your integrity, your character? Be a woman who God can be proud of and smile upon. Know God's Word and interweave it into your life. God's Word provides a solid foundation for one's character, one's integrity, one's moral apparatus, one's lifestyle, one's behaviors, and one's attitude. If you read the last few statements and you responded honestly and said, "No, that does not sound like me, but I want it to be me now," read God's Word, study it, meditate upon it, and walk it out in your life. Before you know it, you will begin to see the transformation take place in your life. Soon, the enemy will be saying, "There she goes. She's on the battlefield for the Lord."

Reflection

_____

_____

_____

_____

_____

Some people won't love you no matter what you do, and some people won't stop loving you no matter what you do. Go where the love is.

Genesis 2:18 says, *"And the LORD God said, It is not good that the man should be alone; I will make him an help meet for him."* To be alone, in a solitary state without companionship, is not part of God's original plan. And, if it was not part of His original plan, it is not part of His plan today. Conversely, love and companionship should not be forced. There is someone in this world for all of us. Someone who will love us with all of our flaws, and someone whom we can love with all of his/hers. Even with this truth, people stay in unhealthy relationships all the time attempting to obtain the love and attention they desire. The reality is- we cannot make someone love us who truly does not. So, stop trying to bend over backwards for someone who was not made for you in the first place.

Reflection

_____

_____

_____

_____

_____

_____

_____

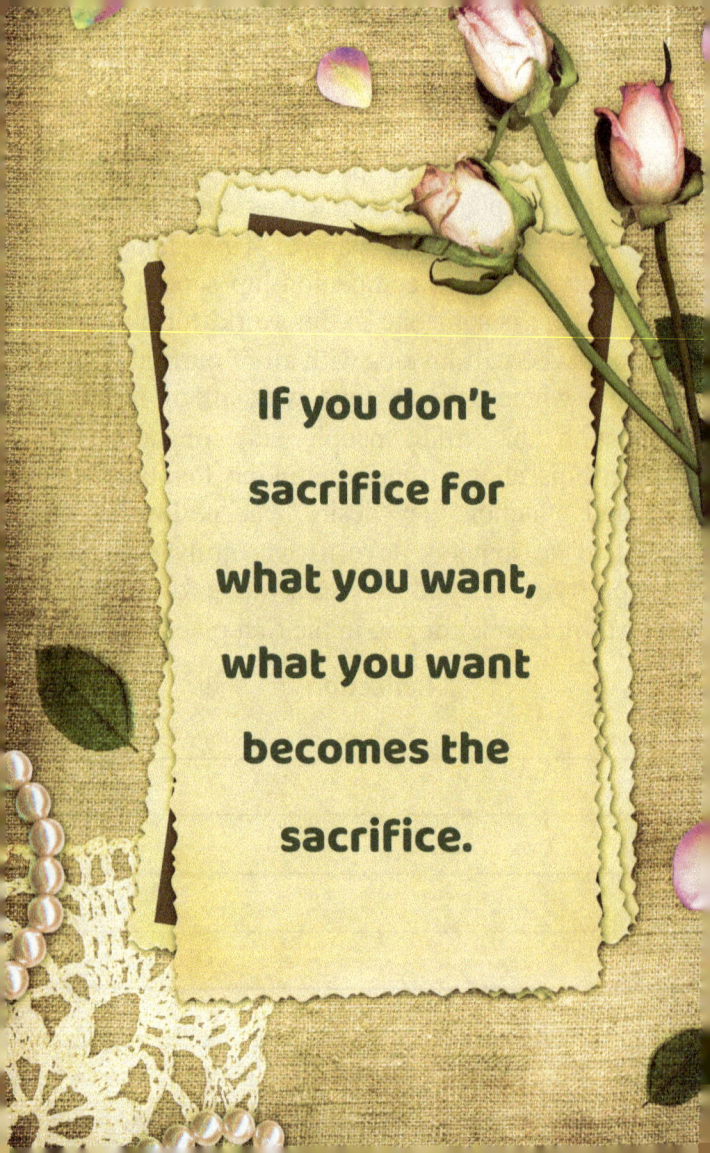

"Anything worth having is worth fighting for," said Susan Elizabeth Phillips. Betty Wright said, "No pain, no gain." I must agree with both of these wise women. It appears that nothing in life comes easily or free. If something is worth attaining, it is going to take some work, maybe even some blood, sweat, and tears. And, it may cost you a sacrifice, which may be less time with family while completing years of study or working longer hours to be able to save enough money for the down payment on a house for your family. However, if you are not willing to make the sacrifice (which may only be temporary) for what you want out of life, then you may end up sacrificing what you want and end up living a life without it.

Reflection

_____

_____

_____

_____

_____

_____

_____

Look back in forgiveness, forward in hope, down in compassion, and up with gratitude.

Zig Ziglar

On a daily basis, we are consumed with all that is transpiring in our life, and we sometimes forget to acknowledge those around us. It is important to step outside of ourselves and focus on others, providing for them the support they need. And, instead of holding grudges for those who have wronged us, we can release them by forgiving their trespasses. In turn, we will have newfound freedom. Rather than walking in despair from all the negativity we have encountered in our lives and holding a bleak outlook for our future, walk in faith, having hope for a brighter tomorrow. Reach out to others in compassion, and always look to the Lord with gratitude for all He has done in our lives.

Reflection

We all have individual needs that must be fulfilled. As we traverse this earth, we seek out those who can assist in filling our needs. We choose jobs that offer the right salary and benefits. We seek friends who have like interests. We fellowship with those who share the same beliefs. But, how do we treat those who do not share much in common with us or who cannot sow into our lives in a tangible or meaningful way? Do we shun their presence, or do we greet them with warmth? Do we smile, or do we turn our head and ignore them? Do we utter a kind word, or do we frown at them? All people deserve respect, love, kindness, and care regardless of their situation, lifestyle, financial status, educational level, or belief system regardless of whether of not they can contribute to our life.

Reflection

_____

_____

_____

_____

_____

_____

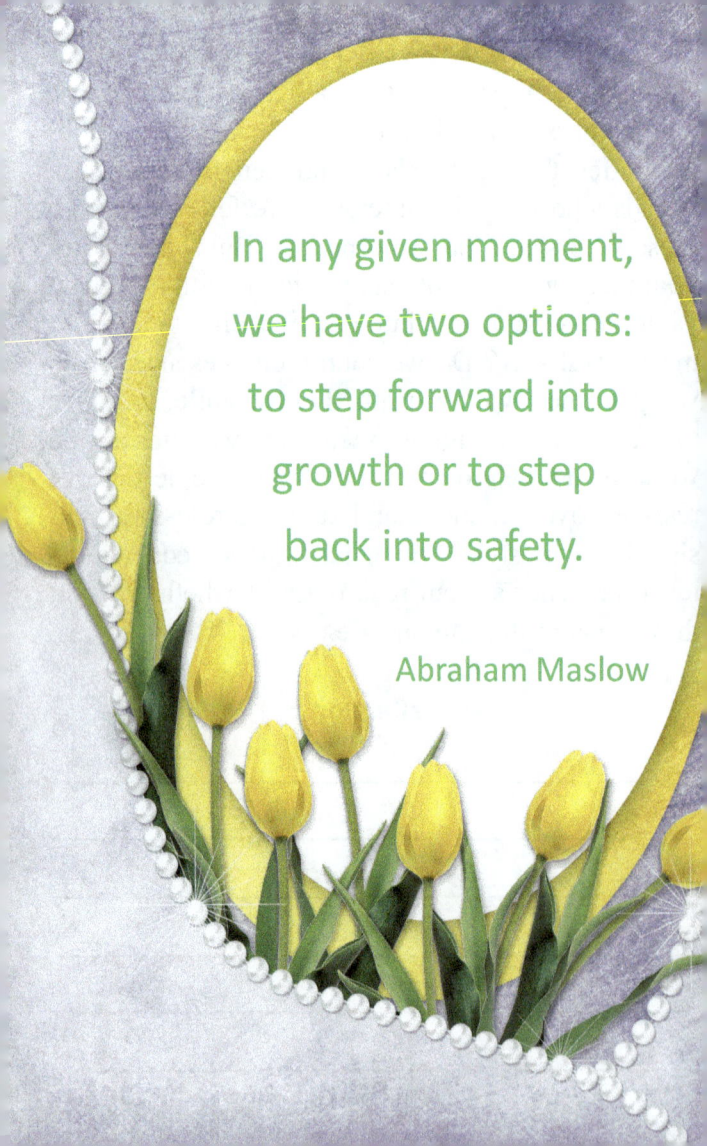

Maintaining the status quo is relatively easy to do and is the most preferred option for most people. Why? Because change can be difficult, and it can bring about feelings of discomfort as a shift is made. Furthermore, change requires adopting a new mindset in order to get out of the current lifestyle you are in or to alter a specific part of your life. To make the choice of whether you should change or not, you need to stop and ask yourself: Is my current lifestyle fulfilling? Am I living up to my full potential? Have I answered the call the Lord has upon my life? Have I achieved my life goals and aspirations? Depending upon how you answer those questions, you will either make the necessary changes or continue to reside in your net of safety and comfortability.

Reflection

_____

_____

_____

_____

_____

_____

_____

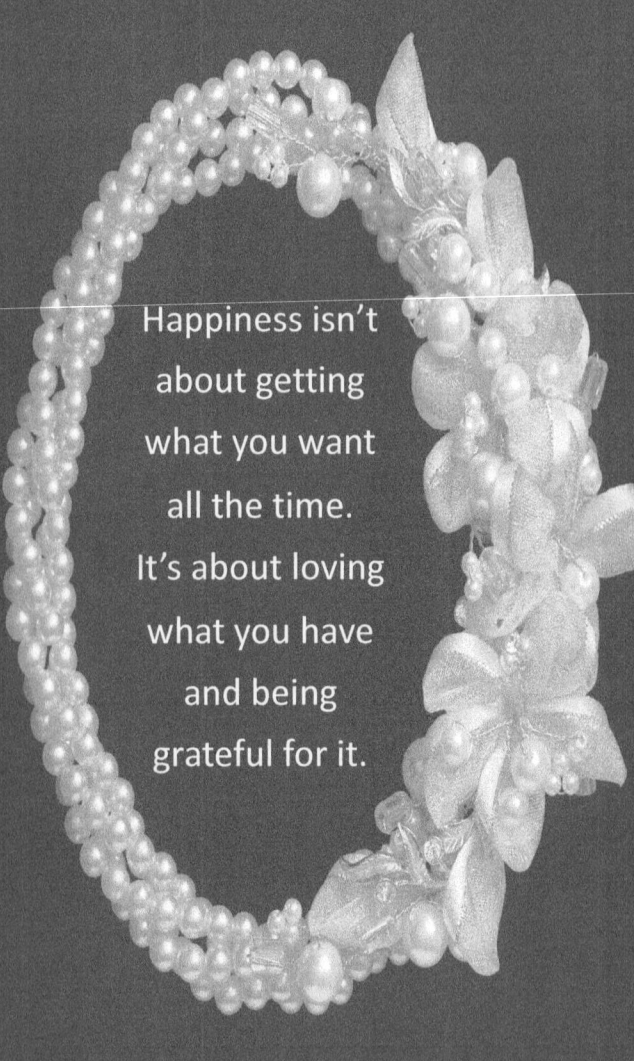

It is human nature to be concerned with self. As part of our human design, we innately consider our personal needs and desires. At times, we will place someone's needs above our own, for example our children, our spouse, our parents, etc. Other times, we allow our desire for happiness to override everything else, and we seek after happiness in different forms. For some, happiness is found in food, so a person chooses to go out for a special meal. For others, happiness can be found in splurging, so a person chooses to buy a new outfit complete with shoes. Happiness means different things to different people. True happiness is found in contentment. God has been truly good to His children, and we should cherish all He has provided for us and be grateful for all He has done instead of always looking for more.

Reflection

_____

_____

_____

_____

_____

_____

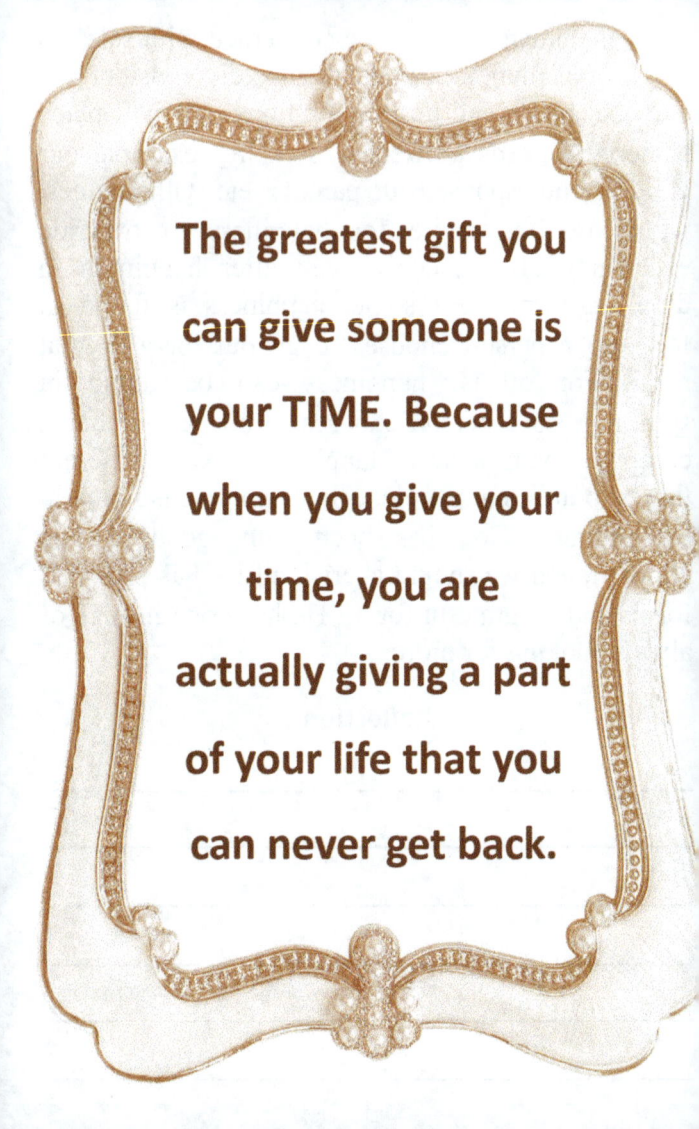

Time is one of the most valuable commodities we have been afforded in the earth realm. We can squander our time, or we can put it to good use. One of the best uses of our time is sharing it with others. Spending time with family and friends allows us to create memories that will last a lifetime. When we look back on those moments, we will laugh, smile, and maybe even cry. So, why not show others how much you love and care about them today by spending precious time with them doing something they want to do. They will never forget the kindness you showed.

Reflection

_____

_____

_____

_____

_____

_____

_____

_____

_____

God is very gracious toward us, and we would be wise to be thankful. Through His providence, He afforded us shelter, nourishment, mercy, kindness, mental and physical capabilities, grace, laughter, love, joy, happiness, fulfillment, financial stability, family, and friends. In His providence also exists shelter, protection, counseling, healing, governance, justice, and peace. God is our all in all, and everything we are concerned about He too is concerned about. A grateful heart is a thankful one.

Reflection

_____
_____
_____
_____
_____
_____
_____
_____
_____

What environment are you surrounded by at this very moment? Where do you exist from day to day? Is your environment conducive to promoting the growth and development you desire for yourself? Is your present mindset regarding your abilities limiting your potential? Does your present income level, education level, or health status debilitate your personal growth? While all of these circumstances that encircle you each day may seem to be barriers to the success you desire, the only true barrier is the one you place in your own path. You and you alone can determine your future goals and aspirations. Do not let the current deficiencies of your present circumstances prevent you from bringing your dreams to fruition. You control the narrative!

Reflection

_____
_____
_____
_____
_____
_____
_____

Today, I want you to focus on all that you are instead of all that you are not.

People will point out your flaws and shortcomings, showing you everything you are not and where you are falling short. The reality though is we all have flaws and shortcomings. Of course, we should want to improve our weak areas; however, we do not allow our weaknesses to overwhelm us or make us feel less than someone who is strong in those areas. In contrast, we have strengths. Those strengths are part of our make up, and we can use them to define who we are rather than using our flaws to define who we are not. *"Therefore I remind you to stir up the gift of God which is in you through the laying on of my hands. For God has not given us a spirit of fear, but of power and of love and of a sound mind"* (II Timothy 1:6-7, NKJV).

Reflection

_____
_____
_____
_____
_____
_____

The minute you settle for less than you deserve, you get even less than you settled for.

Maureen Dowd

Psalm 8:4-6 (NIV) says, *"What is mankind that you are mindful of them, human beings that you care for them? You have made them a little lower than the angels and crowned them with glory and honor. You made them rulers over the works of your hands; you put everything under their feet."* When you understand who you are in Christ and that you were uniquely designed by Him, being positioned a little lower than the heavenly hosts (angels), you will set your expectations for your life within the proper perspective. However, if you allow the enemy to come in and trick you, you will not live up to your God-given potential, and everything God designed for you will be seemingly unreachable.

Reflection

_____

_____

_____

_____

_____

_____

_____

_____

Throughout the various seasons of your life, God has stretched you, developed you, matured you, broken you, healed you, restored you, poured wisdom into you, repaired you, elevated you, revealed His goodness to you, provided you with insight, shared revelation knowledge with you, given you discernment, walked with you, talked with you, enlightened you, loved you, hugged you, smiled upon you, and blessed you abundantly. So, why would you attempt to remain in a space that you have outgrown? Do not allow people to hold you captive in a space that you no longer fit in, a space that is waiting for someone else to fill, a space of development that you have mastered, a space where God has already said, "Well done." If you remain there, your overall growth will be stunted. Allow the Lord to order your steps, for He knows what is best for you.

Reflection

_____

_____

_____

_____

_____

KEEP YOUR **THOUGHTS** POSITIVE BECAUSE YOUR THOUGHTS BECOME YOUR **WORDS**.

KEEP YOUR **WORDS** POSITIVE BECAUSE YOUR WORDS BECOME YOUR **BEHAVIOR**.

KEEP YOUR **BEHAVIOR** POSITIVE BECAUSE YOUR BEHAVIOR BECOMES YOUR **HABITS**.

KEEP YOUR **HABITS** POSITIVE BECAUSE YOUR HABITS BECOME YOUR **VALUES**.

KEEP YOUR **VALUES** POSITIVE BECAUSE YOUR VALUES BECOME YOUR **DESTINY**.

Mahatma Gandhi

How you turn out in life is a direct result of where you place your values. Your values result from what you engage in on a regular basis (habitually) because those are the things that are important to you. Specific behaviors/actions are what led to those regular and ongoing patterns in your life. The actions are a direct result of the words you allowed to slip out your mouth. Before the words were formed, you first had a thought. Proverbs 23:7a states, *"For as he thinketh in his heart, so is he."* Everything begins with a thought, whether the thought came quickly and you quickly reacted or whether the thought came and you pondered about it over much time. Either way, a thought came, an action followed, a habit was formed, the habit transformed into a value, and the value played out in your life. Bottom line- control the thoughts of your mind.

Reflection

_____

_____

_____

_____

_____

Never allow anyone to put an earthly value upon you, such as comparing you to gold, diamonds, platinum, or ascribing you to a monetary value. You are truly priceless in the sight of God, and all manner of men should revere you as such. If you devalue yourself by your words, your thoughts, your actions, your outlook, your demeanor, your thought process, then do not expect others to hold you in high esteem. The way you treat yourself is exactly how others will treat you. According to Ephesians 4:1, you must walk worthy of the calling in which you were called.

Reflection

I want to be a woman who overcomes obstacles in faith rather than tiptoeing around them in fear, one who worships in awe of Your goodness instead of worrying about the what ifs. I want to be a lioness rising up to protect Your children and boldly speaking truth wherever You call me.

We must make a choice about the woman we want to be. Do we possess the boldness to stand in the face of adversity, or do we cower and hide, afraid of what might happen next? Do we praise the Lord as we exercise our faith, trusting He will work on our behalf, or do we tremble with fear of the unknown? If we are women of faith, we walk boldly, trusting the Lord and His Word. He is faithful towards us, and His Word will not return unto Him void. Rather, it will accomplish all for which it has been sent. And, if we walk boldly, demonstrating our faith, we will in turn strengthen another woman's faith by our example. Afterall the Word says, *"as iron sharpens iron, one person sharpens another"* (Proverbs 27:17). Let us look to the Lord for our strength, and once we gather it, let us then be strength for someone else until she gains her own.

Reflection

_____

_____

_____

_____

_____

_____

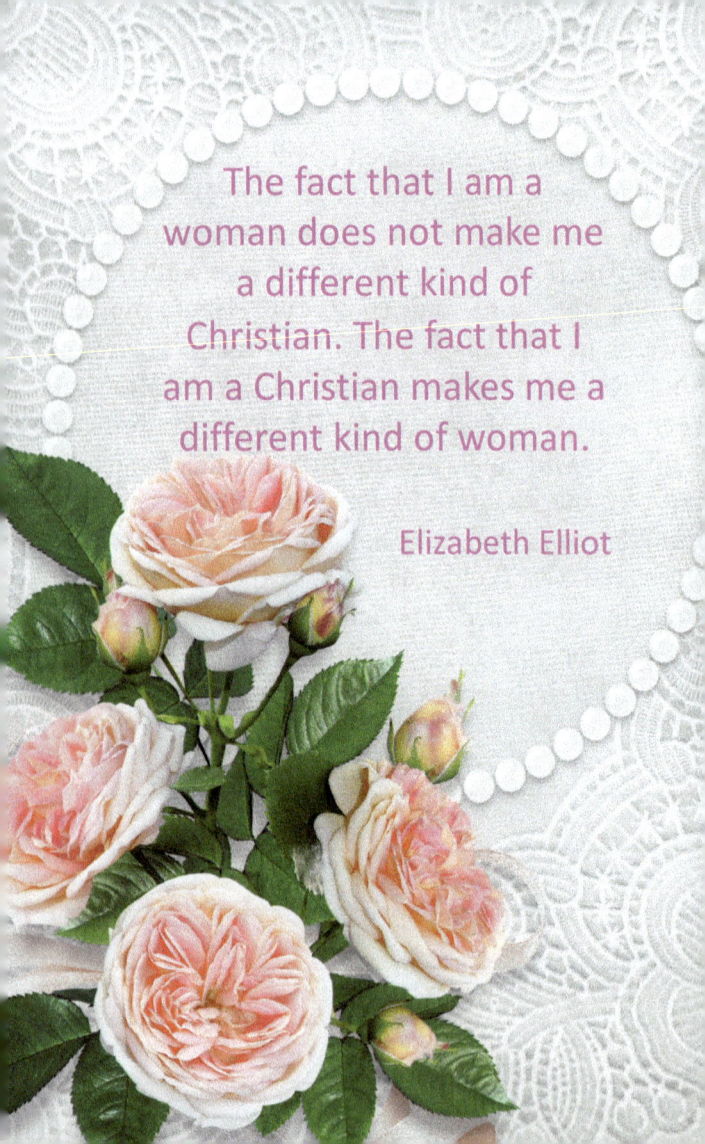

The impact of the Word of God in the life of a woman who is a believer should be readily apparent by onlookers. When people look upon her countenance, they should see the Spirit of God resting upon her. They should witness the joy of the Lord, which is her strength. They should witness a kind-hearted woman who is compassionate toward others. She is one who refrains from engaging in gossip and tearing down her sisters in the gospel. She is one who lends a helping hand to someone in need. She is not swayed by the perspective of others. Instead, she looks to the Lord for guidance. She is a friend to the friendless. She gives hope to the hopeless. She encourages those who are despondent. She raises her hand to lift up the chin of those heads that are hanging down. In everything she does, the light of the Lord shines forth, for she knows she is a child of the King!

Reflection

_____

_____

_____

_____

_____

"Surround yourself with people who are only going to lift you higher."

There are people in your life who will encourage you and provide a support system for you. They will share words of wisdom with you that will provide direction. On the other hand, there are some people who are in your life who unfortunately do not want the best for you. They actually are waiting for you to fail. They may not tell you directly, but if you use spiritual discernment, the Lord will reveal to you who they are. Listen to the Lord's voice. He will show you who is for you and who is not. The next step is for you to draw closer to those in your corner and to separate from those who are not.

Reflection

_____
_____
_____
_____
_____
_____
_____
_____
_____

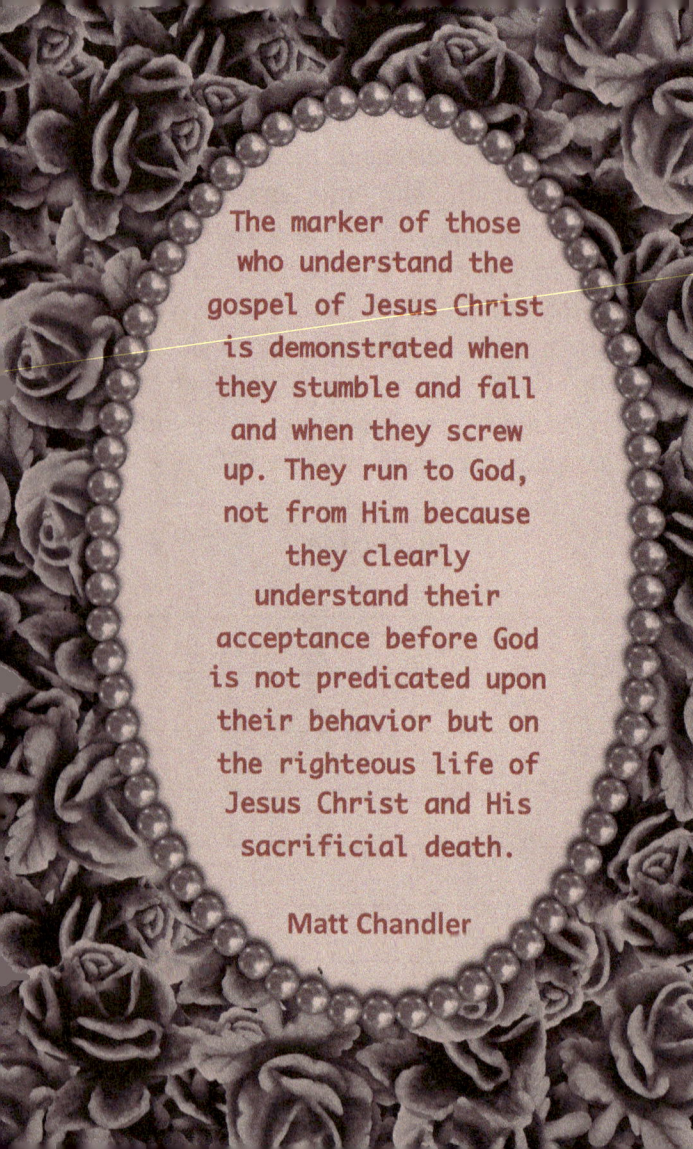

Micah 7:19-20 says, *"Who is a God like unto thee, that pardoneth iniquity, and passeth by the transgression of the remnant of his heritage? he retaineth not his anger for ever, because he delighteth in mercy. He will turn again, he will have compassion upon us; he will subdue our iniquities; and thou wilt cast all their sins into the depths of the sea."* God is a god of mercy, and He is a forgiving god. So, when we experience guilt as the result of our iniquities, we should not try to hide from God. First of all, His eyes are everywhere. There is literally nowhere we can hide. Instead, we should run to Him, so He can give us the strength to break free from what ensnares us.

Reflection

_____

_____

_____

_____

_____

_____

_____

_____

A woman who knows God, cries unto Him in times of distress and celebrates His glory in times of joy. A woman of God neither relies on trends nor her intelligence to change the world. She follows God's plan.

In our everchanging world, trends change from season to season, and it can be difficult to keep up with the changing times. Sometimes, changes occur even faster, such as the stock market. A certain stock that is selling quickly can drop suddenly and vice versa. Our actions are often led by the current trends, and when the trends change, so do our mindset and actions. Living life according to trends and societal perspectives causes people to constantly be in flux and oftentimes unnecessarily. Yes, change is inevitable; however, following the influences of the world system can leave us with undesired results. God has a plan for each of our lives, and we would be wise to follow it. Only God's plan will lead us to our destiny.

Reflection

_____
_____
_____
_____
_____
_____
_____

"For a dream cometh through the multitude of business; and a fool's voice is known by multitude of words."

Ecclesiastes 5:3

Sometimes a person will talk excessively in an attempt to sway his/her audience toward a specific objective. In many cases, the person is just blowing hot air, expelling words that do not yield any gain. Does talking, talking, talking lead one to his/her objective? How could it? To achieve a goal, one is required to engage in the objective at hand. That means putting his/her hand to the plow, working to bring the plan to fruition. Proverbs 29:18 says, *"Where* there *is no vision, the people perish: but he that keepeth the law, happy* is *he."* The individual must first have a plan. Then, he/she must write the plan out in detail, for Habakkuk 2:2 advises us, *"And the LORD answered me, and said, Write the vision, and make it plain upon tables, that he may run that readeth it."* Once the plan is in place, actions must be taken to move the plan forward. The actions must be continued to bring the plan to completion.

Reflection

_____

_____

_____

_____

_____

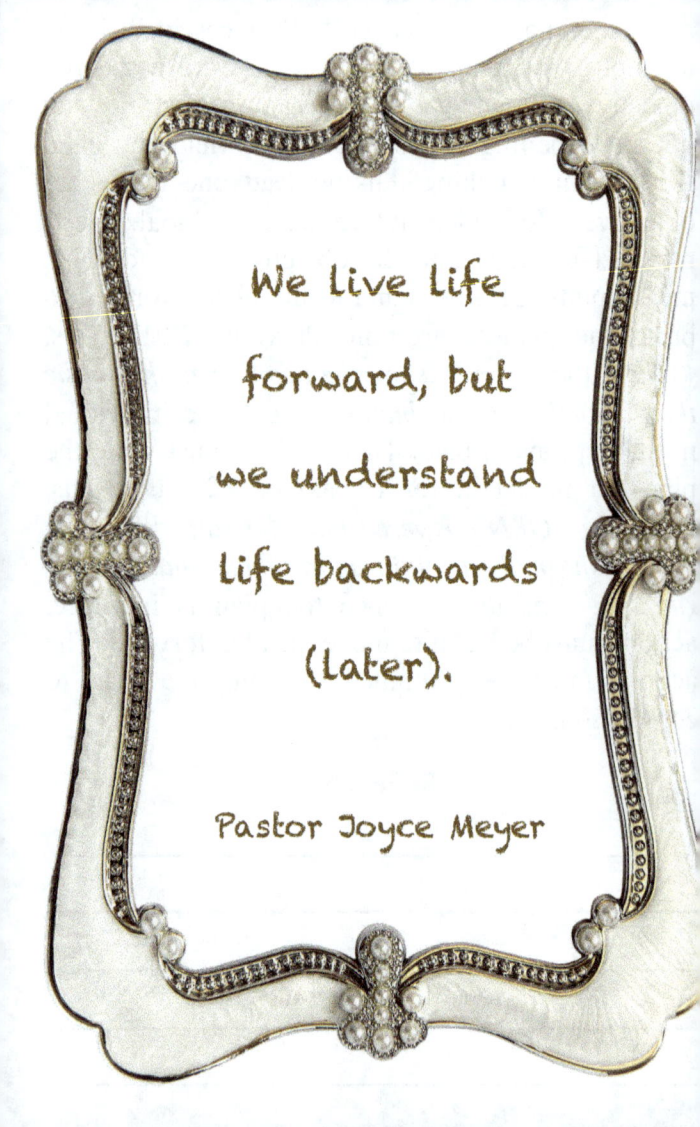

When we are in the midst of life's challenges, we do the best we can with the knowledge and experience we have at that moment. Sometimes, we do not understand why the things that are happening at that moment are happening. We just keep pressing forward until the situation or crisis has been averted. And, just because we may not understand the situation while we are in it does not mean we will not understand it later. When we look in retrospect, we often have a clearer picture and better understanding. Furthermore, just because something hurts does not mean it is bad. And, just because something hurts does not mean God is not working on your behalf. There can be growth as a result of pain. As we continuing living, we should continue learning. It will all come together by and by.

Reflection

_____

_____

_____

_____

_____

_____

WOMEN OF GOD
can never be like women of the world.

The world has enough women who are tough.
We need more women who are tender.

There are enough women who are coarse.
We need women who are kind.

There are enough women of fame and fortune.
We need women of faith.

We have enough greed.
We need more goodness.

We have enough vanity.
We need more virtue.

We have enough popularity.
We need more purity.

There are many characteristics a women can embody. But, ask yourself, "What are the characteristics that a godly woman should behold?" Grace, inner beauty, kindness, gentleness, long-suffering, meekness, love, peacefulness, goodness, forgiveness, self-control, understanding, integrity, wisdom, knowledge, humility, and above all faith. Rather than try to emulate the character of a worldly woman, glean from the godly women that surround you. Also, read the Word of God and learn the characteristics of the women in the Bible that are pleasing to the Father. Then, allow those characteristics to become part of who God is shaping you into.

Reflection

_____

_____

_____

_____

_____

_____

_____

_____

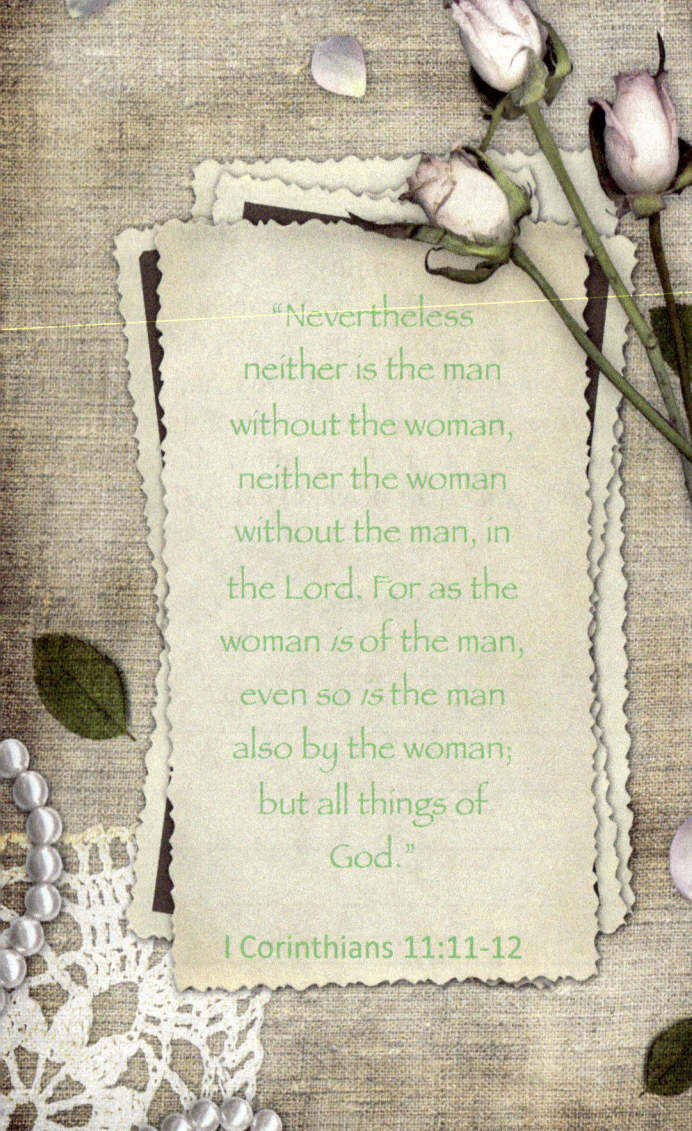

"Nevertheless neither is the man without the woman, neither the woman without the man, in the Lord. For as the woman *is* of the man, even so *is* the man also by the woman; but all things of God."

I Corinthians 11:11-12

All creation is of God, men and women alike. Therefore, it is ridiculous for men to try to outdo or put down women in an effort to render them valueless. The exact opposite is true of women. Women should not attempt to emasculate men in an effort to make them of null effect. We are all valuable to God, and we should therefore value one another. The enemy will use our negative experiences to taint our viewpoint regarding the opposite sex. Remember, that is just one of his tricks. But, you can diffuse the works of the enemy by walking in God's truth.

Reflection

_____

_____

_____

_____

_____

_____

_____

_____

_____

Humility is not thinking less of yourself, but thinking of yourself less.

C. S. Lewis

I Peter 5:5-6 (NKJV) says, *"Likewise you younger people, submit yourselves to your elders. Yes, all of you be submissive to one another, and be clothed with humility, for 'God resists the proud, But gives grace to the humble.' Therefore humble yourselves under the mighty hand of God, that He may exalt you in due time."* Humility can be mistaken for low self-esteem. When a person has low self-esteem, he/she does not know his/her true value. Exercising and demonstrating humility can only be done when a person knows who he/she is and the strengths he/she possesses and has enough self confidence and self assurance that a spirit of pride is not outwardly projected in place of humility. A person who consistently grapples with who he/she is and makes a show of demonstrating and projecting self worth is one who is narcissistic, arrogant, and prideful.

Reflection

_____

_____

_____

_____

_____

_____

"For I know the thoughts that I think toward you, saith the LORD, thoughts of peace, and not of evil, to give you an expected end."

Jeremiah 29:11 (KJV)

When the Lord created each one of us, even before we were formed in our mother's womb, He had our entire life's course already charted. He knew our end from our beginning, every obstacle we would encounter, every trial we would endure, each victory we would experience, each tear we would cry of both joy and sadness, when we would seek Him and when we would retreat. God is an all-knowing god, one who loves us and wants the best for us. Trust Him, knowing He has thoughts of peace towards us and not evil.

Reflection

_____

_____

_____

_____

_____

_____

_____

_____

_____

_____

As fleshly creatures, we are automatically drawn to what we find aesthetically pleasing to our eyes. Although we may attract people with our physical beauty, we will keep their attention longer if we possess an attractive mind that demonstrates our thoughts of concern, an attractive heart that demonstrates our compassion for others, and a beautiful soul that attracts other souls as a result of our concern and compassion. Dare to step outside of yourself, momentarily putting your cares and concerns aside, to show an equal amount of care and concern (and even more- Phil. 2:3) for the wellbeing of another person, especially for his/her soul. Then, watch as the person's life begins to flourish because you dared enough to care and let the light of the Lord within you shine outward.

Reflection

_____

_____

_____

_____

_____

_____

"I have been crucified with Christ; it is no longer I who live, but Christ lives in me; and the life which I now live in the flesh I live by faith in the Son of God, who loved me and gave Himself for me."

Galatians 2:20 (NKJV)

As our faith grows in God, we will surrender our free will unto Him and begin to abide in His will, living for Him and not for ourselves. We will walk according to His Word and ways and not according to our own fleshly desires. Although we continue to reside in the flesh, this earthen tabernacle, we do not allow temptation to take hold and carry us away to fulfilling fleshly desires. To do this, we must crucify our flesh daily as we strive to live for Christ, the One who gave His life for us.

Reflection

_____

_____

_____

_____

_____

_____

_____

_____

_____

_____

"Blessed is she who believed there would be a fulfillment of what was spoken to her from the Lord."

Luke 1:45

According to Hebrews 11:1, *"Now faith is the substance of things hoped for, the evidence of things not seen."* Faith is a matter of believing God's Word to be the ultimate truth without having physical proof. Having faith, one can receive and then accept the promises of God for and into his/her life. Once one has received, accepted, and believed God's promises for his/her life, he/she awaits the fulfillment of those promises as he/she follows God's plan for his/her life. Waiting may include allowing God to align circumstances/situations, clear the path, heal, deliver, and/or mend. Just because we believe we are ready for something to be manifested in our life does not mean it is God's perfect timing. Thus, we must completely put our trust in Him, leaning not to our own understanding, trusting He will deliver on His promises at the right time, in the right season.

Reflection

_____

_____

_____

_____

_____

Here's To The Woman!

...Who knows where she is going
And will keep on until she gets there
Who knows not only what she wants from life
But knows what she has to offer in return.

Here's To The Woman...

Who is loyal to family and friends,
Who expects no more from others
Than she is willing to give

Here's To The Woman...

Who gives the gifts of her thoughtfulness
Who shows her caring with a word of support
Her understanding with a smile
A woman who brings joy to others
Just by being herself.

God created each woman with a unique design. Each one has a different face, personality, character, wit, body shape, shade of skin color, hair texture, etc. Regardless of the physical attributes a woman possesses, she should be confident in who she is, what she wants from life, where she is headed, how she will get there, who she will allow in her corner and on her team, the gifts God gave her, her abilities, and in whom God has called her to be in the earth. Then, she should follow His guidance in getting her to the place(s) He wants her to be all while being thoughtful, considerate, supportive, and understanding to those with whom she will come in contact.

Reflection

_____

_____

_____

_____

_____

_____

_____

_____

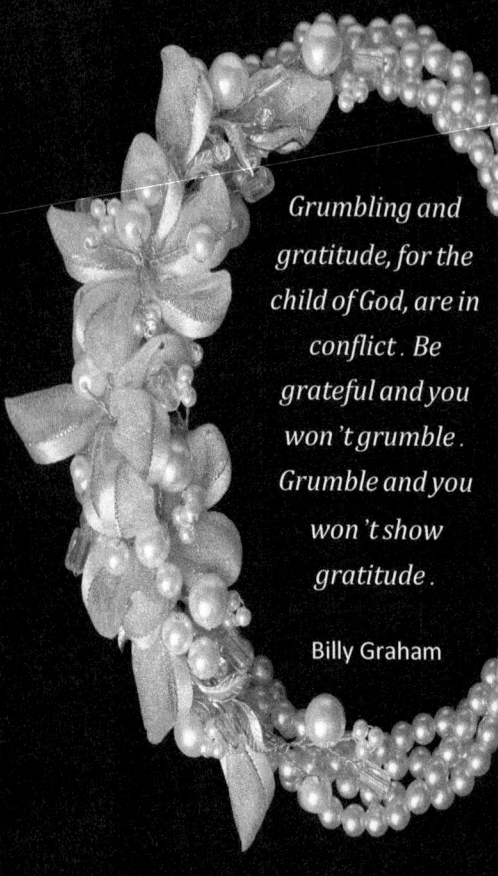

> Grumbling and gratitude, for the child of God, are in conflict. Be grateful and you won't grumble. Grumble and you won't show gratitude.
>
> Billy Graham

Complaining is easy to do even when it is unintentional. Throughout each day, we will hear a series of complaints, while watching television, shopping at a store, while driving and watching other drivers around us who are unhappy with road conditions, and as we interact with family and friends. Because it is commonplace for people to share what they are disgruntled about, it makes it easier for others to get on their soapbox and grumble and complain too. On the other side of the coin of complaints is gratitude. While everything in your life may not be as you would like it, there is much to be grateful to God for. Rather than complain about the few things that are not currently in place to your satisfaction, focus on giving God praise for what He has done. Even when others find things to complain about, you can change the atmosphere by being the one to praise instead. Did you know praise is contagious? Try it and see what happens.

Reflection

_____

_____

_____

_____

Do you really want to look back on your life to see how wonderful it could have been if you had not been afraid to live it?

Carolyn Myss

Life is full of wonderful occurrences intermingled with regrets. You can minimize your regrets by letting go of your fears of failure. If you do not try to achieve your goals, how will you know if you can succeed? If the first attempt does not prove successful, at least you will know what will not work. Maybe on your second or third attempt, you will actually achieve your goal. However, if nothing ever works, at least you can say you tried, and you will not have to live wondering 'what if?'

Reflection

_____

_____

_____

_____

_____

_____

_____

_____

_____

_____

Faith tells me, no matter what lies ahead of me, God is already there.

Often times, when we think about what lies ahead in our future, trepidation will grip our heart. Because of life's uncertainty, the future can seem scary. But, God has already charted our course. He will always be with us every step of the way, even unto the ends of the world (Matthew 28:20).

Reflection

Trying to walk each day as a woman of faith, while facing all this world has to throw at us, is sometimes almost unbearable. But the Lord has promised He will never leave us or forsake us. And along the way, He often sends into our life the blessing of a *special sister in Christ.*

Having friends is special, but having friends who are women of God, who share the same beliefs as you, have the same standards as you, honor, reverence, and worship God as you, who will stand in your corner, hold your hand when you cry, listen when you just want to talk, is a blessing afforded us by God Himself. He knows what we need, who we need, and when we need them. Bless the Lord for sisters in the Gospel.

Reflection

Be the kind of woman who does not spend her days worrying about the future because she knows what does or does not happen this week, this semester, or this year, God will still fulfill His purpose for her.

When God gives you a plan for your life, it will come to fruition in His timing. So, do not be dismayed if things do not appear to line up and fall into place when you think they should. If God gave you the vision, He will bring it into manifestation. Be steadfast and unmovable while you are staying the course. Have faith because God's words will not return to Him without accomplishing what He intended.

Reflection

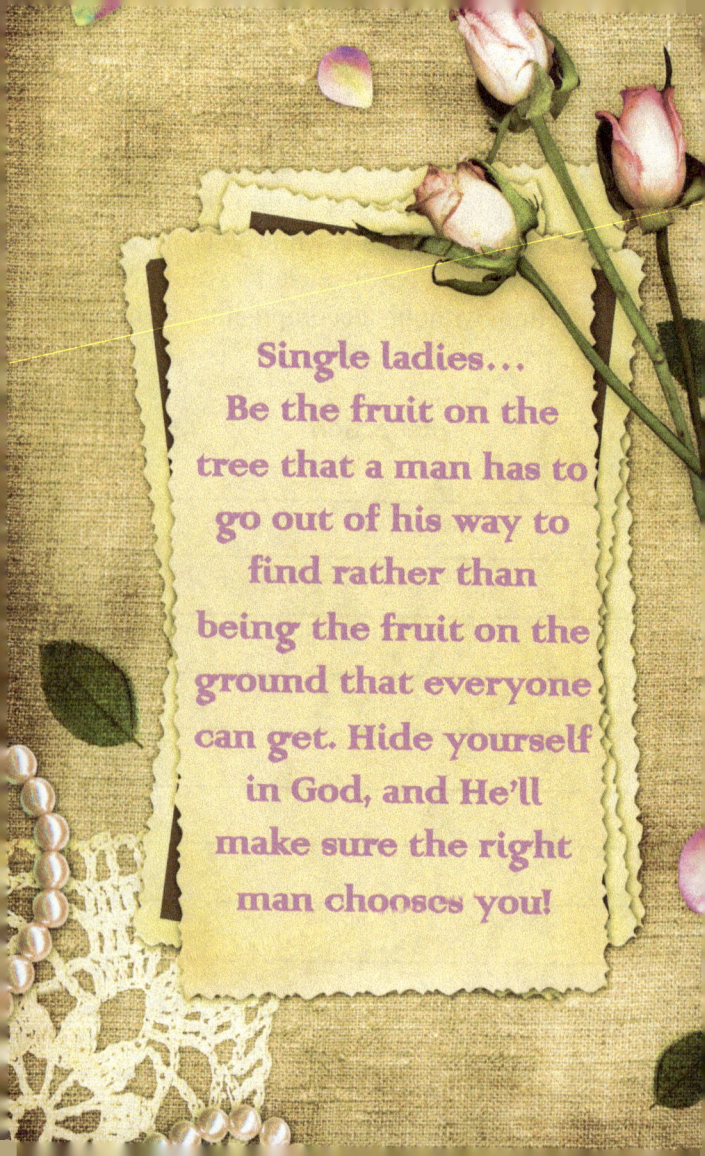

Philippians 4:6 (ESV) admonishes, *"Do not be anxious about anything, but in everything by prayer and supplication with thanksgiving let your requests be made known to God."* Women of God, there is nothing wrong with desiring a mate. Being in a hurry to have a mate can lead to catastrophe. Allow relationships to manifest in God's timing if you truly want the best outcome. God already designed someone specifically for you. In due season, his path will cross yours.

Reflection

When a woman veils her body in modest clothing, she is not hiding her body from men. On the contrary, she is revealing her dignity to them.

A woman's attire speaks volumes and will evoke certain responses from those around her, whether desired or undesired. I Timothy 2:9-10 says, *"Likewise also that women should adorn themselves in respectable apparel, with modesty and self-control, not with braided hair and gold or pearls or costly attire, ^{10} but with what is proper for women who profess godliness - with good works."* The attire you choose to adorn yourself with will speak volumes to others about who you are on the inside.

Reflection

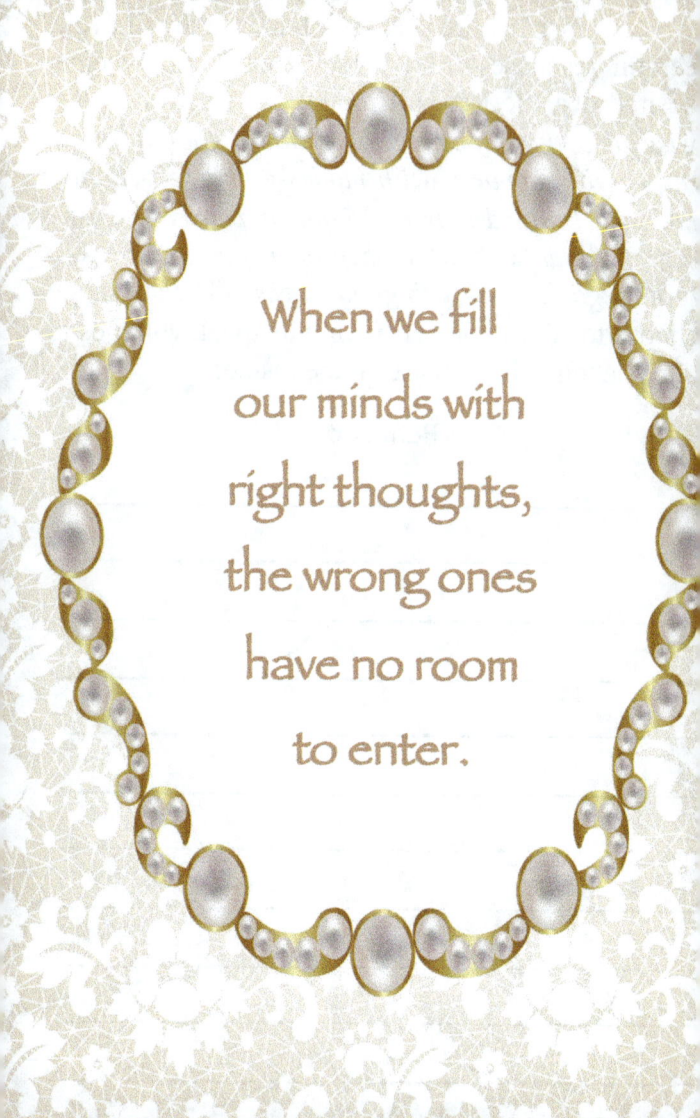

When we fill our minds with right thoughts, the wrong ones have no room to enter.

Philippians 4:8 (NIV) admonishes, *"Finally, brothers and sisters, whatever is true, whatever is noble, whatever is right, whatever is pure, whatever is lovely, whatever is admirable - if any-thing is excellent or praiseworthy - think about such things."* Evil thoughts, thoughts of ill repute toward others, disgruntled thoughts, bitter thoughts and the like will attempt to creep into your mind and take up residence. If you entertain them a beat too long, they will do just that. Instead, take Apostle Paul's advice. Think about all that is positive, not allowing negativity the right of way.

Reflection

_____
_____
_____
_____
_____
_____
_____
_____
_____

It is not what you do for your children, but what you have taught them to do for themselves that will make them successful human beings.

When women are blessed to give birth to children, the women become responsible for nourishing them, protecting them, clothing them, cleaning them, loving them, teaching them, and being role models for them. The lessons mothers teach their children should not only help them to navigate the world they live in today, but the world they will live in tomorrow and the world their own children will live in someday. What our children learn from us, either directly or indirectly, can and will impact their future.

Reflection

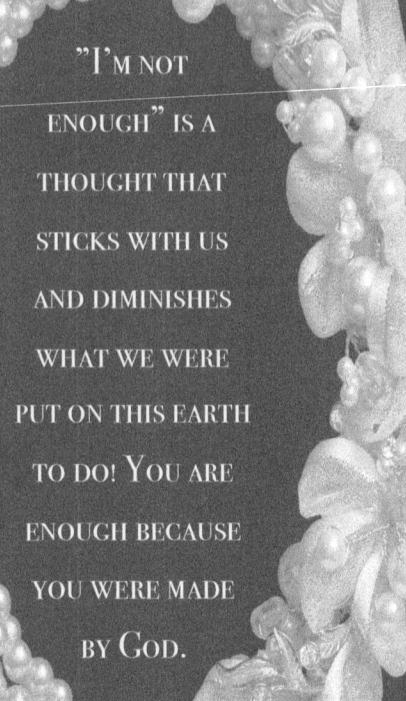

"I'm not enough" is a thought that sticks with us and diminishes what we were put on this earth to do! You are enough because you were made by God.

Someone lied to you either when you were a little girl, in a relationship, or both by telling you that you were no good, never going to be anything, or not smart enough. The sad reality is you bought into the lie and carried it around with you, allowing it to define who you are. Let's correct the lie right now. You are good enough. You are valuable. You are smart. You are worthy. God created good things, and one was you!

Reflection

I am a Daughter
-who was loved before I was born
I am a Sister
-to those in God's family
I am a Friend
-to the greatest friends in the whole world
I am a Student
-of teachers who help me achieve
I am a Helper
-to those in need
I am a Princess
-to the King of kings
I am a Treasure
-to the Lord of lords
I am a Child
-of the heavenly Father
I am a Soul
-saved by grace through Christ Jesus
I am a Christian!

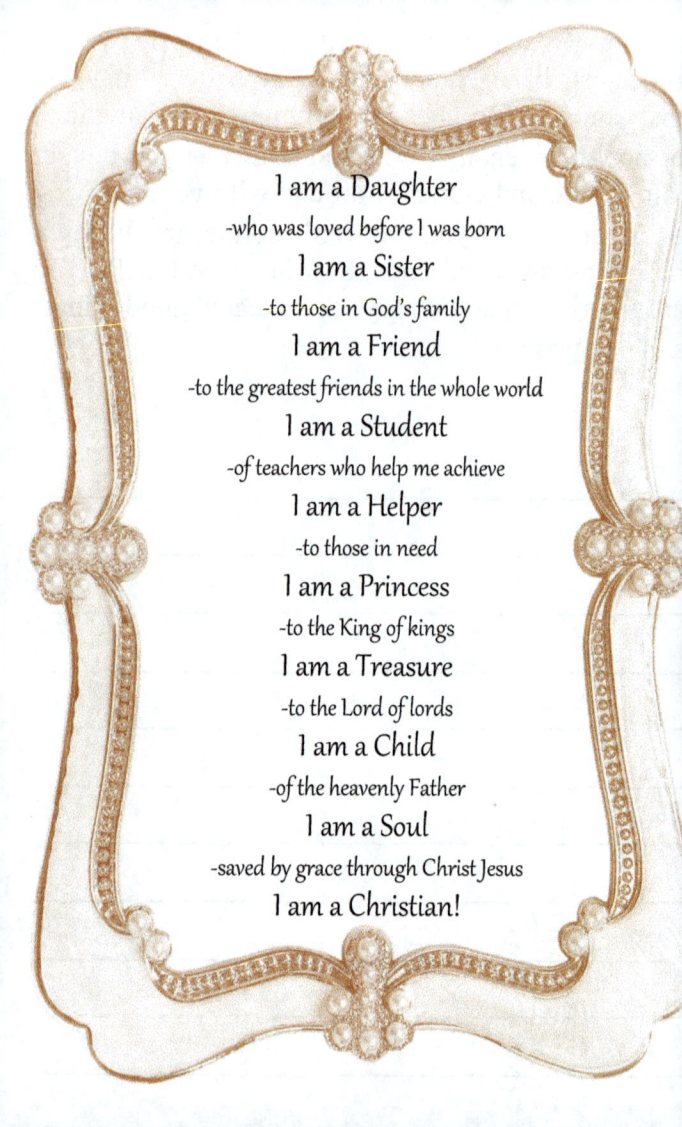

As women, uniquely created and designed by God, we fulfill many roles: daughter, mother, wife, aunt, sister, teacher, leader, business woman, child of God, student, friend, etc. Which role means the most to you? Is it the earthly role of a mother, a sister, or a friend? Or, is it the spiritual role you fulfill (that will lead you into eternity) that holds the most value for you? If you really think about it, the role of a Christian, being the daughter of the most High God, will allow you to be more effective in all your other roles. Right?!? So, value all your roles, and be successful in all of them.

Reflection

_____

_____

_____

_____

_____

_____

_____

_____

Anyone can find the dirt in someone. Be the one that finds the gold.

"He who earnestly seeks good finds favor, But trouble will come to him who seeks *evil,*" Proverbs 11:27 (NKJV). Don't be the one to go around digging for people's skeletons that have been buried or tucked away. Everyone has a past, and there are some secrets they do not want anyone to know. Respect that. Mind your own business. Rather than being a busybody, search for the positivity a person possesses, allowing them to shine in the eyes of their peers.

Reflection

We don't need to compress ourselves into an imitation of what everyone else is doing in hopes to fit in. We already fit in where we belong: in the palm of the Creator.

We are uniquely designed by the Almighty God. He did not create us to be identical to others by acting the same, by having the same personalities, by having the same goals, by having the same thoughts, or by having the same style. Therefore, we should not try to become a carbon copy of someone else. Dare to be the individual God created you to be even if you have to stand alone while doing it. You are in a class of your own. Be proud of who you are - in Him!

Reflection

*Woman of God:
Some days may feel impossible to make it through. But get up, show up, and be up. God's strength will arise within you. His peace will uphold you. His power will sustain you. You are an overcomer!*

Christie Williams

This life is much like a roller coaster ride. There are high points, and there are low points. The high points are exciting, but the low points (the valleys) can be difficult to bear. The valleys can even cause deep-seated depression that may lead to an unwillingness to get out of bed, to face the day, to deal with challenges, or to eat. I admonish you to muster up the strength to rise above the circumstances. Take one step at a time, and after you take the first step, you will be able to take the second. As you go, God will overtake you and propel you forward. You can do this!

Reflection

_____
_____
_____
_____
_____
_____
_____
_____

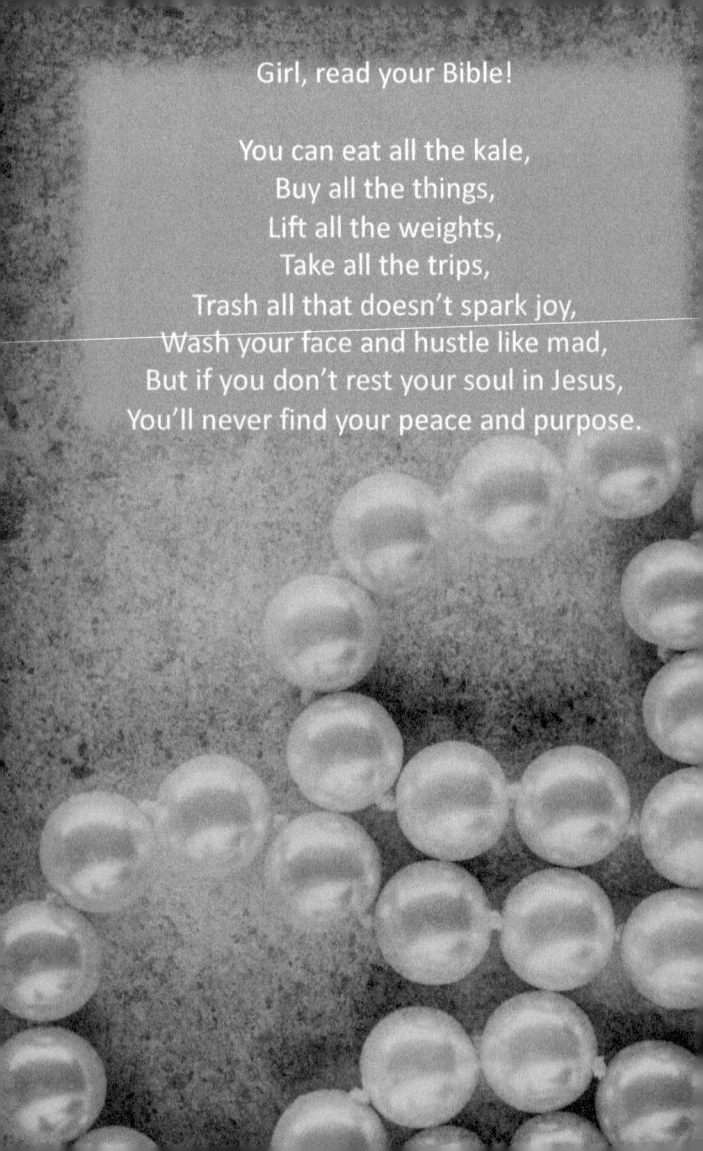

Mark 8:36 (NLT) says, *"And what do you benefit if you gain the whole world but lose your own soul?"* We spend much time attending to our physical appearance and running the rat race of commercialism in this capitalistic society. We enjoy the pleasures of this life without fail. Jesus did say He came so we may have the abundant life. However, we cannot neglect our spiritual nourishment, which is found in God's Word. Just as we attend to our physical and emotional wellbeing, we too must attend to our spiritual wellbeing.

Reflection

_____

_____

_____

_____

_____

_____

_____

_____

_____

_____

Stop shrinking to fit into places you have outgrown.

Furaha Joyce

I Corinthians 13:11 (NLT) says, *"When I was a child, I spoke and thought and reasoned as a child. But when I grew up, I put away childish things."* From the time you were born, you shifted from one position to another. As a believer, God is still shifting you. He will elevate you, change your patterns, remove people from your life and you from theirs. He will develop you and give you a craving for more of Him. Meanwhile, you may sometimes resist the change and continue hanging out with those He has removed from your life or engaging in activities you no longer desire. Change may not always be comfortable, but it is certainly inevitable. Allow God to bring about growth and development in you. Receive it. It is for your good.

Reflection

_____
_____
_____
_____
_____
_____
_____

Your enemies will get what is coming to them. Unclench your fist, shut your mouth, and remove anger from your heart. Walk the path of righteousness, and let God fight your battles. Never forget who you are. Amen.

Psalm 105:15 says touch not God's anointed nor do His prophet any harm. The anointed of God have a special protective covering, and if anyone should breach God's shield, he/she must answer to the Almighty. So, as God's anointed, step back. Do not attempt to fight fire with fire. Do not provide an open door for Satan to enter and to cause more havoc in your life. According to Matthew 5:44, there is a method for dealing with those who attempt to come against us: *"But I say unto you, Love your enemies, bless them that curse you, do good to them that hate you, and pray for them which despitefully use you, and persecute you."*

Reflection

_____
_____
_____
_____
_____
_____
_____
_____
_____

3 Things

I don't know much
But 3 things I do
There is a God
His Word is true
Stay close to Him
He'll see you
through.

Stay focused on God. Trust Him, for His Word is true. Walk in His ways and His statues. He will never fail you.

Reflection

And one day, she discovered that she was fierce and strong, and full of fire and that not even she could hold herself back because her passion burned brighter than her fears.

Mark Anthony

When the day comes that you realize the full and true essence of yourself, nothing will be able to stop you from coming into your own and realizing who you are, your true self as God created you. When the epiphany manifests, go forward into your destiny!

Reflection

_____
_____
_____
_____
_____
_____
_____
_____
_____
_____
_____
_____
_____
_____

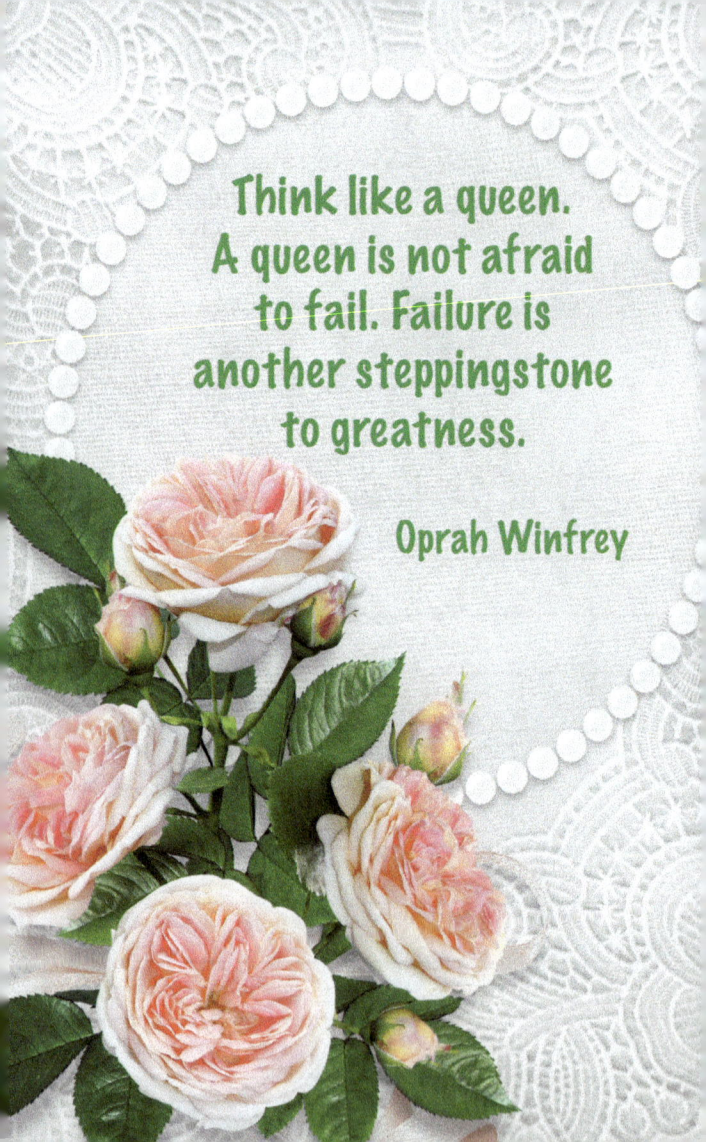

As a young girl, you were a princess, learning who you are from all the women who surrounded you and spoke into your life. As a woman, you are now a reigning queen, taking possession of all God has granted her. Until you know your rightful place, you will not be able to break free from the ties that bind nor will you be able to move forward to where God is calling you, a place where He has already predestined you for greatness.

Reflection

We all have a unique journey that no one else can make for us or take from us. Encapsulated within the journey is a unique story, one about a unique woman. Sharing your story in your authentic voice is powerful, not only for you but for those who hear and receive it. Revelation 12:11b says, *"and they overcame him by the word of their testimony."* Satan is defeated when you open your mouth and share with others your journey, your triumph, your victories in the Lord. That is how powerful your testimony is. Be free to share who you are and your experiences, so other women can triumph with you, as they blossom within their own life.

Reflection

_____

_____

_____

_____

_____

_____

_____

_____

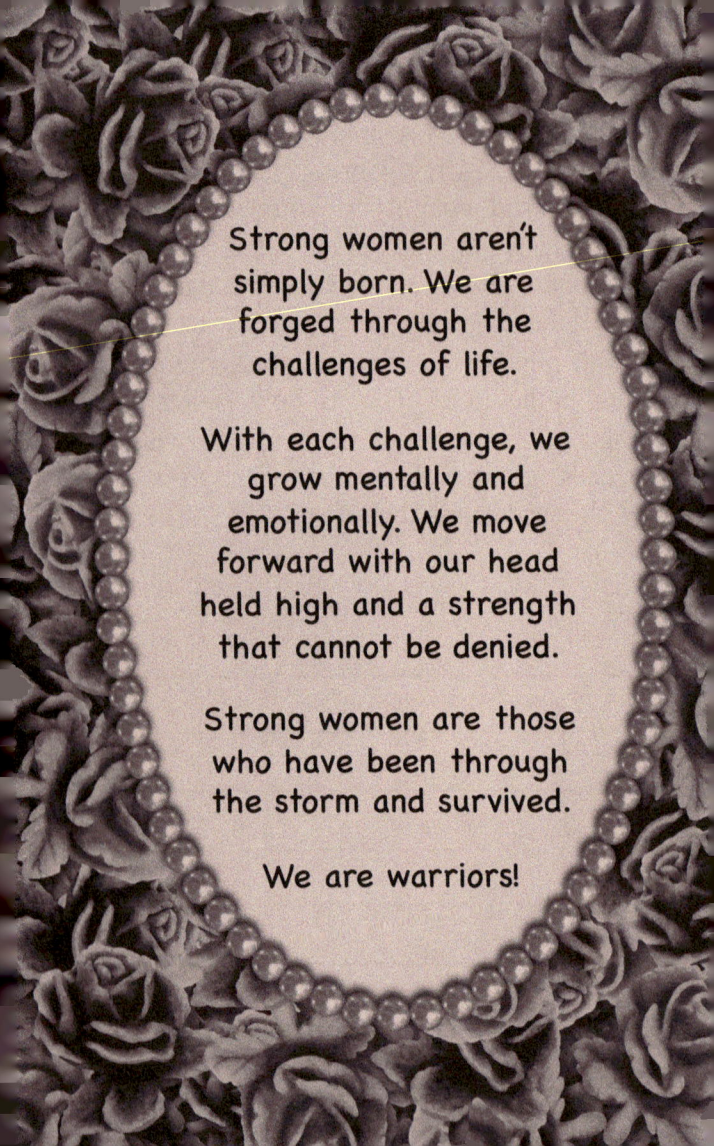

It is often said, "What the devil meant for evil, God will turn it around for our good" (Genesis 50:20). During many of the trials you went through, you thought or said, "Lord, why me?" Sometimes, you even questioned whether or not you would truly make it through the storm. But, now you look back, realizing God was always there, and He carried you through. He was there when you dealt with heartache, breakups, death, financial struggles, health challenges, and so much more. Through it all, you found your strength. You are stronger now than you ever were before. Now, you can counsel others. You can be the rock they lean on. You can be the voice of wisdom when others are experiencing times of trouble. Woman, you are a warrior. Continue to stand on the battlefield.

Reflection

_____

_____

_____

_____

_____

_____

Every storm is part of YOUR journey. YES, you will make it through this one, too. You will come out stronger than you were before…

Heather Stillufsen

No one ever volunteers to go through a storm, but should you find yourself in one, muster up the courage to face it head on. Allow God to show you the solution for navigating your way through. Don't be like the Israelites who found themselves in the wilderness for 40 long years. Don't be stiff necked and act as though you are hard of hearing. Attend your ears to hear what thus says the Lord, and allow God to order your steps. Remember, His Word is a lamp unto our feet and a light unto our path (Psalm 119:105).

Reflection

Be a strong woman, so your daughter will have a role model and your son will know what to look for in a woman when he becomes a man.

Children habitually emulate what adults model before them. Inevitably, children will learn habits, both good and bad. And, they will make decisions about their present and their future based on what they learn from what goes on around them. A strong mother who presents herself as good role model (by making sound decisions, treating others with dignity and respect, taking care of her home and family, walking in integrity and self respect, all while being loving and kind) will in essence, demonstrate to her daughter how to be a strong woman who is well respected by those around and in the community. She will demonstrate to her son the character of a woman that he will in turn seek after when he begins his search for a wife, the future mother of his children.

Reflection

_____

_____

_____

_____

_____

_____

_____

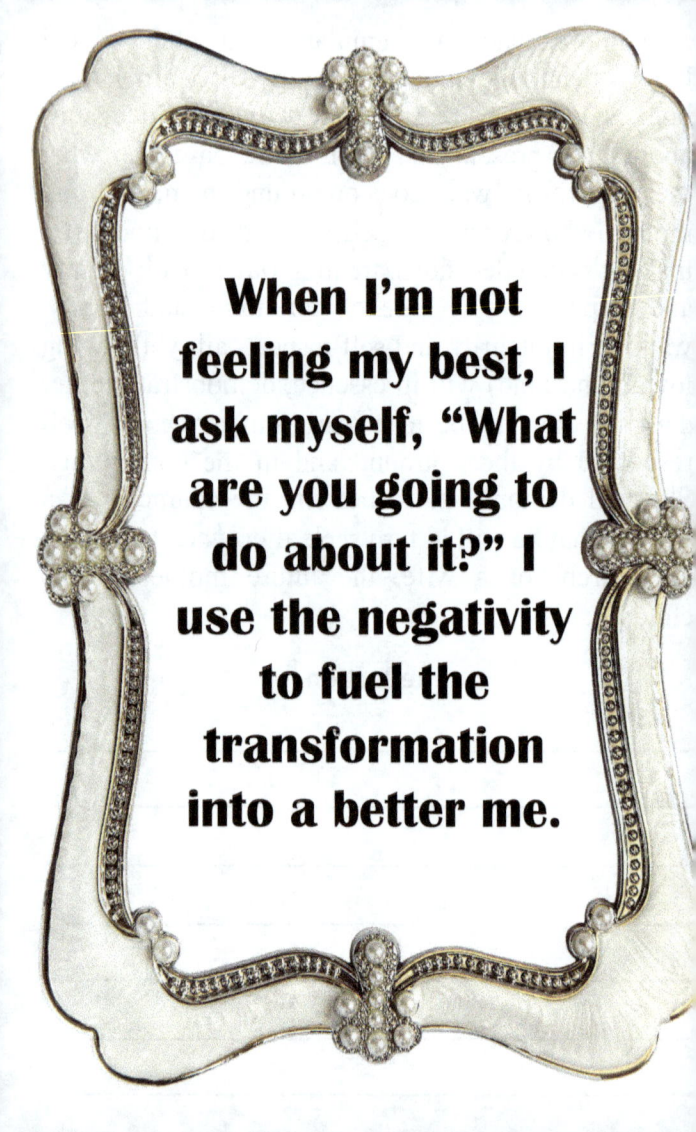

When I'm not feeling my best, I ask myself, "What are you going to do about it?" I use the negativity to fuel the transformation into a better me.

Wallowing in self pity does not solve anything. Engaging in a pity party only accomplishes one thing: wasting valuable time. If ever you feel as though you are not on top of your game and making the moves you desire, stop and think about the plan of action you have in place. Is your plan actually effective? Is it going to achieve your desired goal? If not, give your plan an overhaul after you re-assess it. Sometimes, we don't want to admit that our plan is faulty or at least parts of it. However, being honest with ourselves can help us out of a rut and back onto the right track of moving our life forward. Transforming our thinking can lead to transforming our plans, which leads to being proactive and accomplishing our goal, while feeling better about ourselves.

Reflection

_____

_____

_____

_____

_____

_____

_____

Growth is about *you*. Don't set a goal for anyone else. If it's not going to actually get you something you want, remember you can walk away. That time and energy might be better spent on figuring out what your goals actually are.

Jane Scudder

Every woman has the personal responsibility of fulfilling her God-given assignment. The best way to do that is by setting goals: short term as well as long term. In the midst of completing goals, we are constantly developing and maturing. Maturing to the next level is what assists in our success of completing the next goal on our list. In the interim of achieving our list of goals, other people will request our participation in extraneous activities, which may detract from what we are attempting to accomplish. If the extraneous events distract us from achieving our goals, we need to weigh our involvement in them carefully, so as to not get off course. If we do not stay focused, it will take longer to accomplish what we have our hearts set on.

Reflection

_____

_____

_____

_____

_____

_____

_____

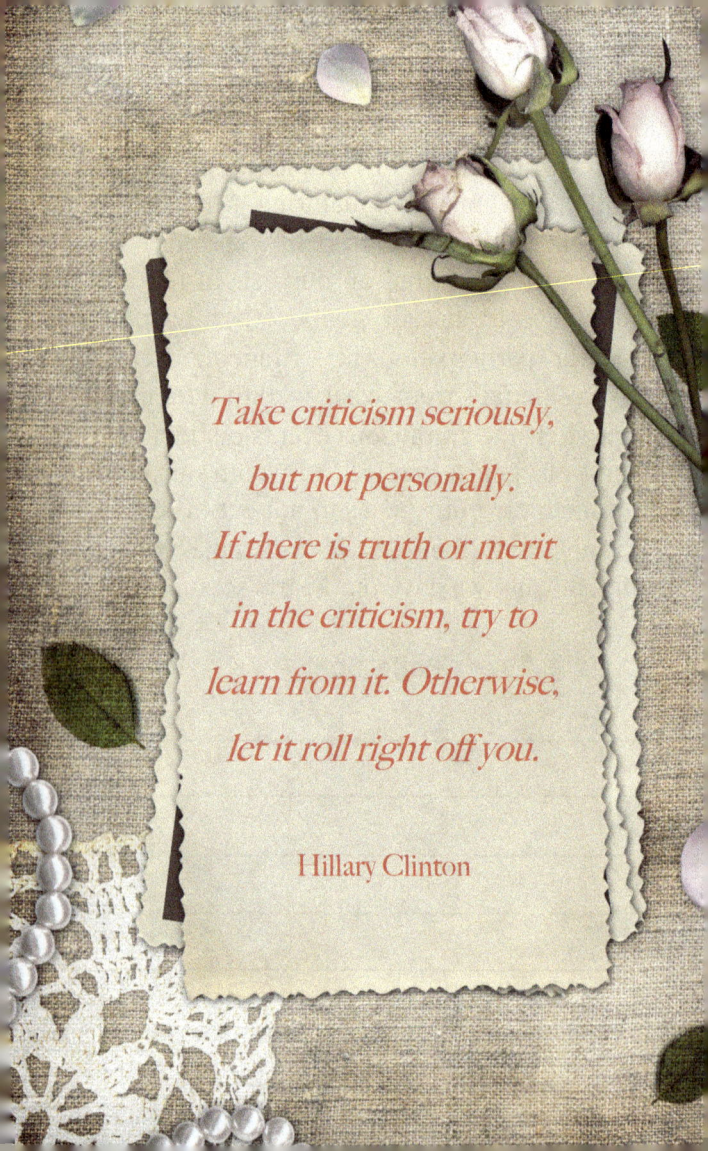

Everyone is a critic these days. Some people offer their critiques because they actually want to help you improve yourself. Others critique you because they have nothing better to do, and oftentimes, they just want to make you feel bad about yourself. If you find a criticism has merit, take heed to it by making the necessary changes. If it does not, ignore it. Do not give it energy it does not deserve.

Reflection

We all make mistakes, have struggles, and even regret things in our past. But you are not your mistakes, you are not your struggles, and you are here NOW with the power to shape your day and your future.

Dr. Steve Maraboli

Our past and the mistakes that occurred are not meant to define us. They are meant to teach us valuable lessons to shape who we will become in our future. We are only the sum total of our mistakes if we continue to make them or focus on them, giving them power over us. If, instead, we learn from them and change for the better by letting go of bad habits and not allowing our past to consume us, our future will be brighter. The choice rests in our hands. Let go of excuses, and take control of your life by leaving the past in the past and seizing the opportunity of today!

Reflection

_____
_____
_____
_____
_____
_____
_____
_____

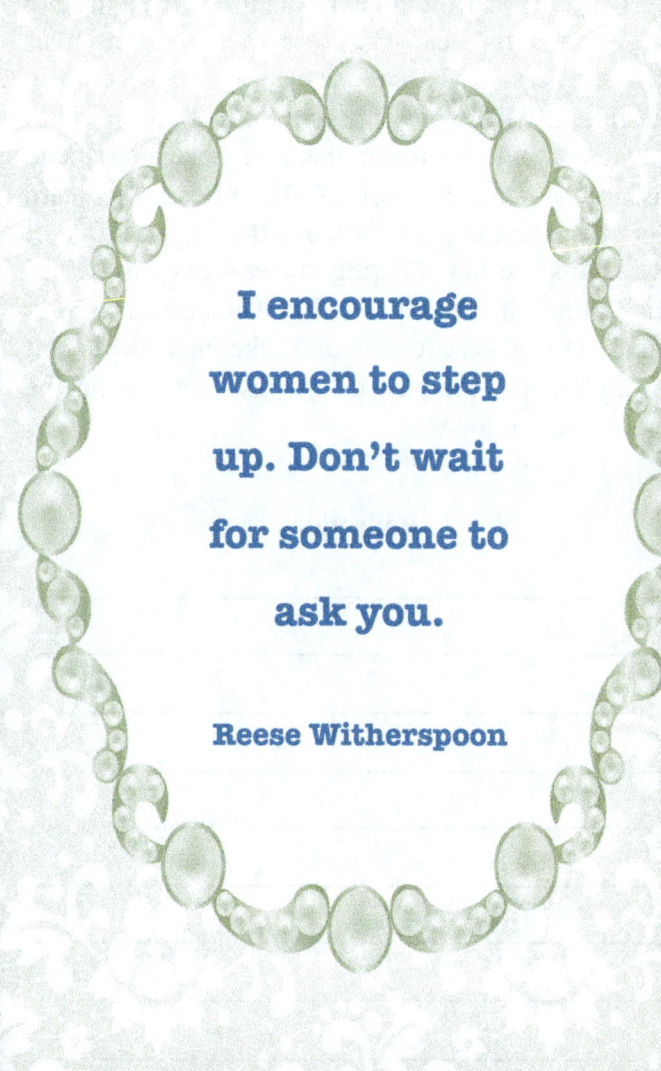

I encourage women to step up. Don't wait for someone to ask you.

Reese Witherspoon

God gave each woman a voice and talents. If you have the ability to handle a task or to assist someone in need, you should step up and fill the need. You do not need to to wait until someone solicits your assistance before you decide to be instrumental in accomplishing tasks. They may not know you have the skill set to complete the task, so why not volunteer and make life easy for all involved? If you are afraid of being rejected and that is what is preventing you from coming forward and volunteering, ask God to remove the spirit of fear from you. What would make you feel better: staying quiet to avoid rejection or offer your gifts and talents to fulfill a need?

Reflection

_____
_____
_____
_____
_____
_____
_____
_____

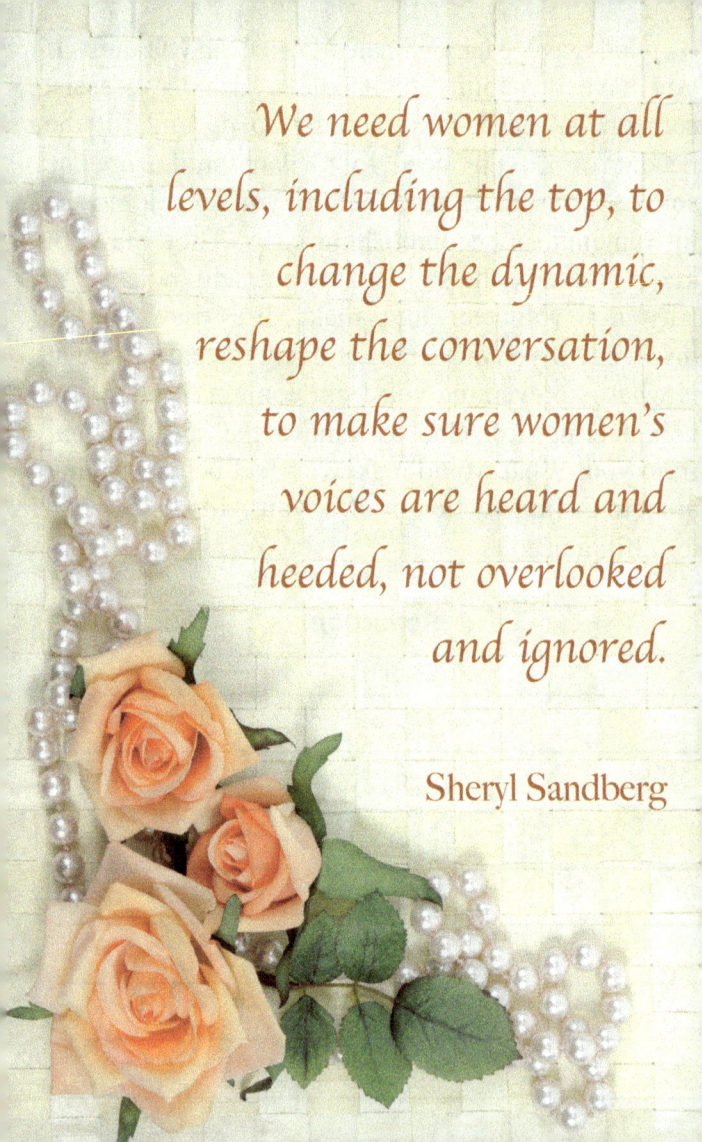

> We need women at all levels, including the top, to change the dynamic, reshape the conversation, to make sure women's voices are heard and heeded, not overlooked and ignored.
>
> Sheryl Sandberg

Women can be instrumental in all organizations and are needed at various levels within those organizations. Unfortunately, as a result of women being treated as second-class citizens, which was never God's intent, women have had to fight for their natural born, God-given rights. The fight for equal and fair treatment is still being pursued today. However, with women in positions, doors can be opened to other women who can then help to reshape the culture in a positive manner as they participate in conversations that will lead to meaningful change for all people.

Reflection

_____
_____
_____
_____
_____
_____
_____
_____
_____

> If you see something that is not right, not fair, not just, you have the moral obligation to do something about it.

Congr. John Lewis

Your voice is powerful, maybe more powerful than you realize. You can use your voice to effectuate change in your community, within your circle of influence, within your workplace, and even in the world at large. With technological advances where they are today, you don't have to wait for an audience to gather for you to share what's on your mind. You already have an audience waiting on social media platforms: Facebook, Instagram, TikTok, etc. Just choose one, or use them all. So, when you witness injustice taking place, refuse to remain silent. Speak up on your own behalf and on behalf of others, especially the downtrodden, the disenfranchised, the marginalized, the imprisoned, and the seemingly forgotten.

Reflection

_____
_____
_____
_____
_____
_____
_____

The success of every woman should be inspiration to another. We should raise each other up. Make sure you're very courageous: be strong, be extremely kind, and above all be humble.

Serena Williams

When one woman achieves her goal, advances in her career, begins a new business, or succeeds in any area in her life, the women who surround her or hear about her success should celebrate her victory as their own. This world is not always user friendly for women, and women fighting against one another, trying to hold each other back will inevitably hold all women back. So, instead of spreading negative energy, let's rally together and support one another. Doing so will propel more women forward and higher at a more rapid pace. Upward and onward, women!

Reflection

_____
_____
_____
_____
_____
_____
_____
_____
_____

I did not get there by wishing for it or hoping for it, but by working for it.

Estée Lauder

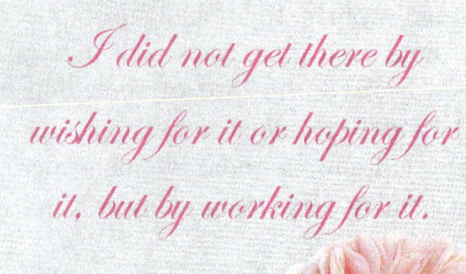

James 2:17 says, *"In the same way, faith by itself, if it is not accompanied by action, is dead."* This verse can also be made applicable to goals you hope to attain. Attaining your goal can only be done by putting in the necessary work. To make your goal attainable, break it into smaller, more manageable goals, and get started. Before you know it, your overall goal will be attained.

Reflection

The world system has taught us to compete with one another. If you ever participated in sports, you competed against the opposite team. In academic competitions in school, you competed against other students. Women compete with other women in a variety of areas for a variety of reasons. The truth of the matter is while competition can be healthy at certain levels, overall, competition is unhealthy because it causes undue stress, which oftentimes leads to other conditions: mental, physical, and emotional anguish. When the time comes for you to come out of your shell, do it and do it without worrying about trying to outdo the next person. You are your own person. Just do you!

Reflection

_____
_____
_____
_____
_____
_____
_____
_____

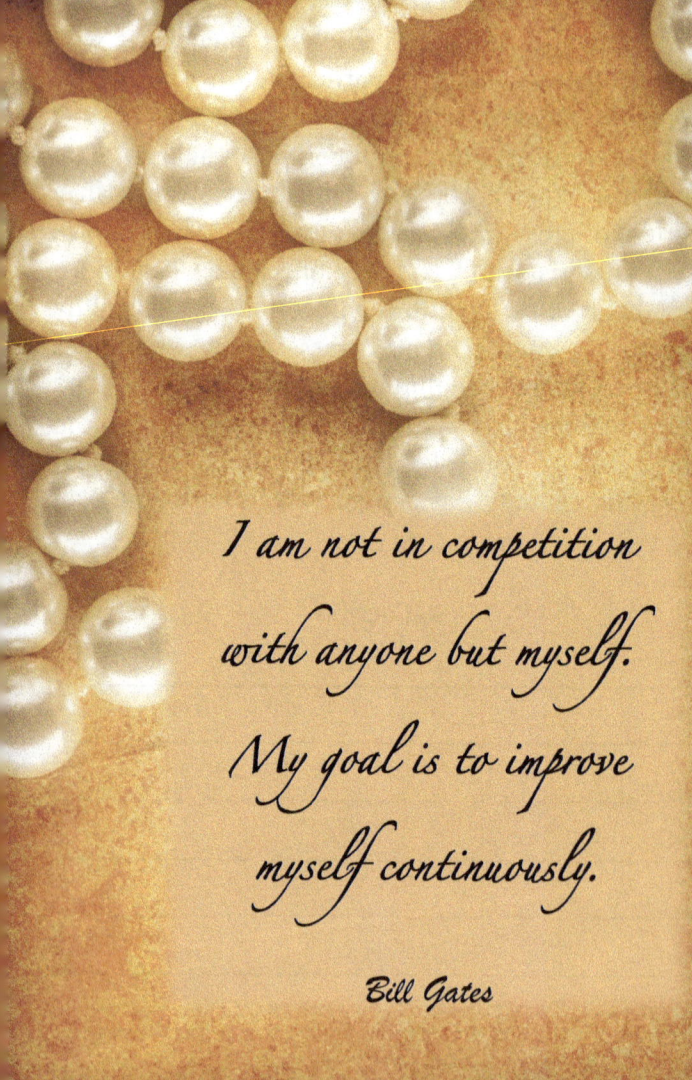

Everyone should be concerned with self improvement, and it should not be in connection with comparing yourself to someone else. First of all, you don't know what position the person was in before she elevated to the place she is now. Secondly, you don't know what she had to go through to get where she is. Therefore, you don't know if you can even make it to where she is. What if you do not possess the proper tools or skill set? When you are looking to improve your situation, you should only compare yourself to yourself. Be the best person you can be according to how God made you and your personal abilities. Never allow anyone to make you feel bad about where you are in life according to where they think you should be. Assess yourself and be satisfied. If you are not satisfied, take action and make improvements according to your own standards.

Reflection

_____

_____

_____

_____

_____

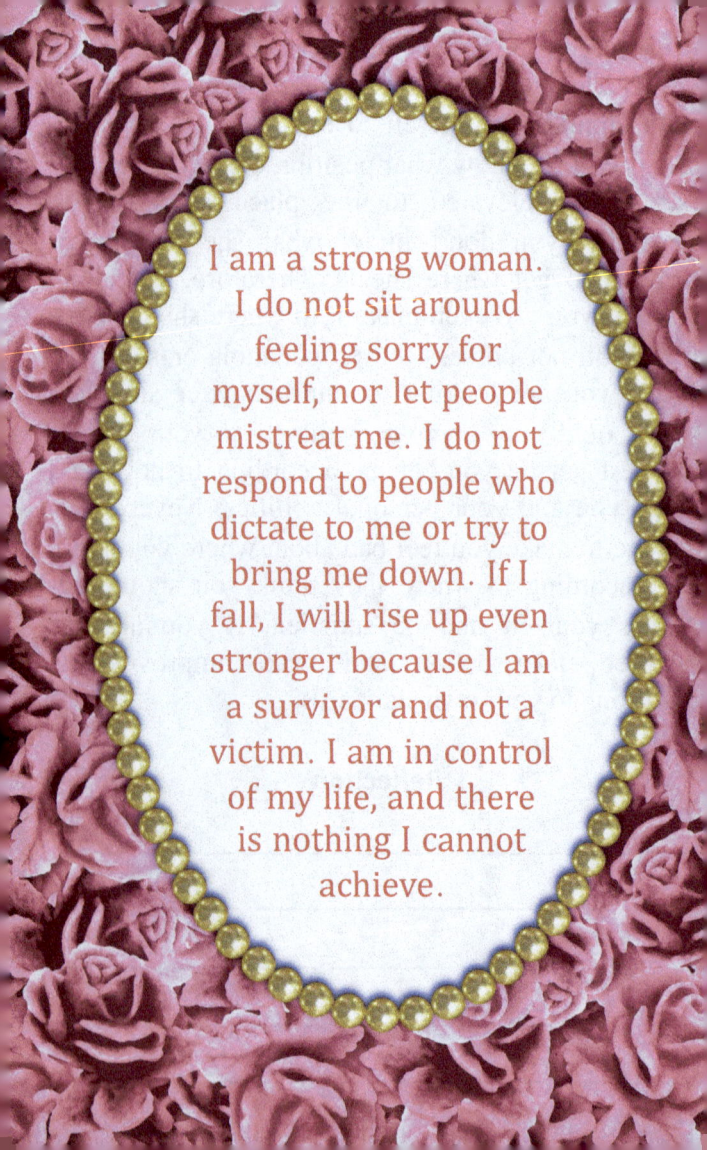

You are in control of your life and the choices you make, whether right or wrong, wise or foolish, healthy or unhealthy, good or bad. Whatever decision you make, be willing to deal with the consequences of your actions. If you make a decision that did not pan out the way you anticipated, don't let it get you down and don't allow others to put you down. Rise above the choice and move forward. Life is a learning process. Be dedicated to learning and growing on your own terms. People are not required to agree with you or like your choices. Don't live to please others. You are the only one who has to live with you every minute of every day. After all decisions have been made, make sure you can live with yourself.

Reflection

_____

_____

_____

_____

_____

_____

_____

A strong woman is one who feels deeply and loves freely. Her tears flow as abundantly as her laughter. She is both soft and powerful and is both practical and spiritual. In her essence, a Strong Woman is a gift to the world.

A strong woman is one who is confident in herself. If she is heartbroken, she shows it, even if it means openly shedding tears. If she is happy, she doesn't mask her smile because others are down. She demonstrates her true emotions, so everyone can see her authentic self. Her authentic self is a powerful woman, who is a gift to mankind.

Reflection

When a female is young, she is immature physically, mentally, and emotionally. Naturally, she engages in immature thinking, which leads to immature behavior. As she matures physically, her behaviors and thinking <u>should</u> mature as well. As she shifts developmentally, she leaves unhealthy competitions behind because she comes to realize they only serve to separate rather than bring together, demote rather than elevate, and discourage rather than encourage. Now, as a woman, she prefers to empower and promote other women, assisting them in being all they can be.

Reflection

_____
_____
_____
_____
_____
_____
_____
_____
_____

When you set your sights on moving higher, whether it is in the corporate arena, in your educational pursuits, in leadership, or wherever God is calling you, while that shift may come with an increase in salary, your main focus should be on how many lives you can impact in your new position. Also, as you experience elevation, evaluate if it is feasible to take others with you. Remember, there is room for advancement for all of us. We just have to be willing to see the value in others.

Reflection

I am an example of what is possible when girls from the very beginning of their lives are loved and nurtured by people around them. I was surrounded by extraordinary women in my life who taught me about quiet strength and dignity.

First Lady Michelle Obama

We can all look back to see how we were raised, who we were raised by, and who influenced our lives. Some of our character traits were learned from those women. What qualities do you possess that you can pass on to the young women of the next couple of generations. What impact can you have on their lives? What characteristics can you demonstrate before them that they can assimilate into their own character and one day demonstrate before other women?

Reflection

_____
_____
_____
_____
_____
_____
_____
_____
_____
_____
_____
_____

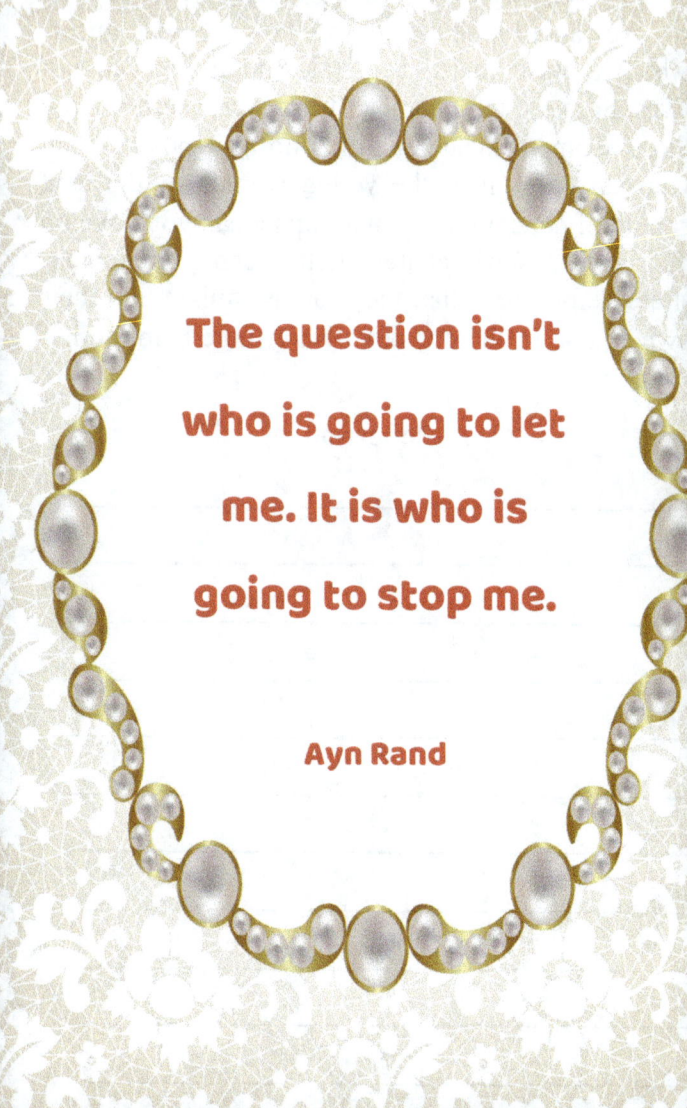

We have been conditioned to seek permission for nearly everything in life: from our parents, from our teachers, from our employers/supervisors, from our spouses, and from society in general in the form of acceptance. When it comes to the calling God has placed upon our lives, we do not need to seek permission from mankind. We need to walk in obedience to the instructions God has given us for our lives. It is Him, and Him alone, whom we will need to give an answer to on Judgment Day. Remember, obedience is better than sacrifice (I Samuel 15:22).

Reflection

_____
_____
_____
_____
_____
_____
_____
_____
_____

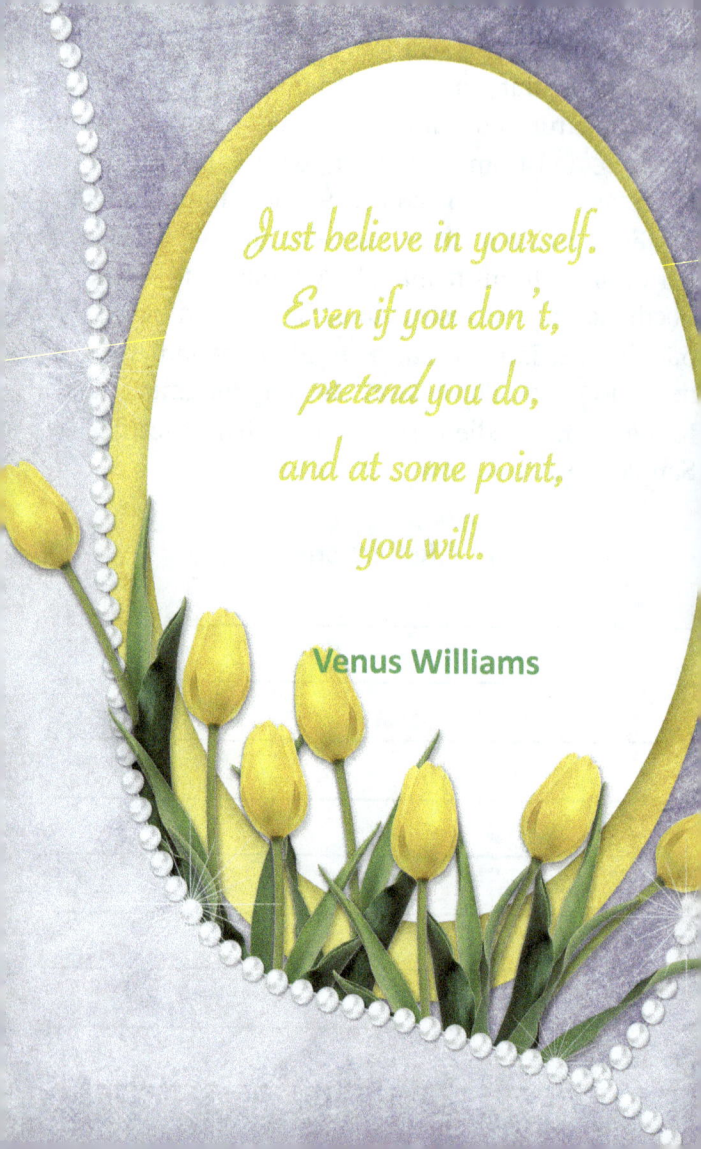

According to Romans 4:17, we must begin to view our situation in the spirit rather than the natural, speaking things into existence that have yet to materialize. When we fail to believe in ourselves, we can expect to accomplish nothing. Conversely, when we have faith in God and the abilities He has blessed us with, we can be free to believe in ourselves as well as our aspirations, knowing they will come to pass just as God has promised us and pre-ordained them to be. Be encouraged, and speak life into a seemingly dead or hopeless situation.

Reflection

Gift of Salvation for Non-Believers

"For all have sinned, and come short of the glory of God." (Romans 3:23)

This section was written especially for non-believers, those who have not accepted the gift of salvation. The gift of salvation saves souls from eternal damnation and is a free gift offered by God Himself.

John 3:16-18 says, *"For God so loved the world, that he gave his only begotten Son, that whosoever believeth in him should not perish, but have everlasting life. For God sent not his Son into the world to condemn the world; but that the world through him might be saved. He that believeth on him is not condemned: but he that believeth not is condemned already, because he hath not believed in the name of the only begotten Son of God."*

This section of scripture tells us God's purpose for giving His son Jesus to the world. The world was in a bad condition. The world was overwrought with sin; the people were living for fleshly desires rather than for God's desires.

As a result of the world's conditions, God decided He would offer the perfect sacrifice that would save the world from being a place where people were lost and had no hope. He decided His own son could stand in proxy for the sin-filled world, taking all sin upon Himself.

So Jesus came, born of a virgin, to save this dying world. He walked on this earth for 33 ½ years, doing the work of His Heavenly Father. At the appointed time, He died by way of crucifixion upon a cross at Calvary, on Golgotha's hill. He shed His blood and died for you and for me. Because His blood was pure, it paid the penalty for all unrighteousness and gave those who believe in Him direct access to His father's throne.

Scripture tells us in Matthew 27:51 that the veil of the temple was ripped in two from top to bottom, at the moment that Jesus' spirit left His body. As a result of the veil's removal, we are no longer required to have a high priest make intercession for us. We, as the children of the Most High God, are able to approach the throne of God for ourselves, and Jesus sits on the right hand of the Father making intercession for us.

But what is even more miraculous than God offering His own son as the perfect sacrifice was the fact that when Jesus was placed in grave clothes and placed in a tomb, He only remained there until the third day. God would not have it that His son would remain in the heart of the earth forever. In order for people to believe in the awesome power of God and His dear son Jesus, a miracle had to be performed. So, on the third day, after Jesus died on the cross, He was resurrected, demonstrating the omnipotence of God.

This very act was the act that would cause people to believe in a god that reigns supreme and holds the power of the universe in His very hands, a god that could save them from themselves.

Today, if you are an unbeliever, you can change your destiny. You can change where you will spend your eternity. Our Heavenly Father gives us the freedom of choice about how we want to live our life here on earth and how we want to spend eternity. In Deuteronomy 30:19, God boldly declares, *"I call heaven and earth to record this day against you, that I have set before you life and death, blessing and cursing: therefore choose life, that both thou and thy seed may live."*

So, dear friend what choice will you make today? Will you spend your eternity with the Creator or will you suffer Hell's eternal flames? Again, the choice is yours. Just as the men aboard the ship who were with Jonah became believers, you too can make a choice to accept the only one and true living God as your god.

If after reading the above passages, you have decided that you want to spend your eternity in Heaven with God, the creator, and His son Jesus, and the Holy Spirit, read through what has affectionately come to be known as the Roman's Road. This is the road to salvation. As you read through the scriptures that comprise the Roman's Road, you will also read the explanation for each scripture, so you will have clarity about what you are reading and confessing.

The Roman's Road to Salvation

The road to salvation begins with Romans 3:23 which declares, *"For all have sinned, and come short of the glory of God."* This scripture explains that everyone has come short of God's glory and needs redemption. Then, Romans 6:23a states, *"For the wages of sin is death."* Here, we learn that the consequence of living a life of sin is death. Everyone will experience physical death as a result of the sin committed in the garden of Eden, but those who commit themselves to a life of sin will suffer eternal damnation in the lake of fire (Rev. 19). Continue with the rest of verse 6:23 that says, *"but the gift of God is eternal life through Jesus Christ our Lord."* There is an alternative to suffering eternal damnation. We can accept the gift of salvation by accepting Jesus as our personal Lord and Savior. Then, Romans 5:8 says, *"But God commendeth his love toward us, in that, while we were yet sinners, Christ died for us."* We are able to receive the gift of salvation because Christ came to earth and shed His blood for us on the cross.

Continue to Romans 10: 9-10 which says, *"That if thou shalt confess with thy mouth the Lord Jesus, and shalt believe in thine heart that God hath raised him from the dead, thou shalt be saved. For with the heart man believeth unto righteousness; and with the mouth confession is made unto salvation."* If we confess with our mouths that Jesus is the son of God, that He came and died for our sins, and that God raised Him from the dead, we will receive salvation.

Finish with Romans 10:13, which states, "*For whosoever shall call upon the name of the Lord shall be saved.*" Call upon the name of God by saying these words, **"Lord Jesus, come into my heart and save me, Lord. I believe that you are the Son of God who came and died on the cross for my sins. I believe that you rose from the grave. I also believe that you now sit in heaven on the right side of the Father, making intercession for me. I accept you as my Lord and my Savior."**

Now that you have confessed with your mouth that Jesus is the son of God and that He died for our sins and rose from the grave, **YOU ARE NOW SAVED!!!!** You will spend your eternity in heaven.

The next step is very important- you must find a Bible-based church that teaches the Word of God and confesses the Lord Jesus Christ to be the son of God. Don't delay. Do this immediately. Do not leave yourself open to the enemy. Get connected with the saints of the Most High God and keep yourself covered with the unspotted blood of the Lamb.

Here is my prayer for you.
Father God,

I thank you for the opportunity to minister your word to the unsaved, the unchurched, and the uncommitted. Father God, I pray now for the souls who have just received the gift of salvation. Lord Father, they have opened their hearts to you, and I know that you have received them into your kingdom and written their names in the Book of Life. Father God, I pray that you will touch their lives and show yourself mightily before them. Let their eyes be opened by the scales falling off, allowing them to see clearly.

Father God, I even pray for the backslider, those who have turned away from you after receiving the gift of salvation. You said in your Word that you desire that none would perish. So Lord, I send your Word to them right now, praying that they would confess the iniquity in their heart, repent, and turn from their evil ways, so that they may receive a life of abundance. You said in your Word in Matthew Chapter 14, that every knee shall bow before you and every tongue will confess that Jesus is Lord.

Father God, I pray now that we all come under subjection to your Word and that we will humbly submit our lives to you. I ask all these things in the name of my Lord and Savior Jesus Christ.
Amen, Amen, Amen!!!!

I will continue to pray for your success in your walk with God. Remember, this spiritual walk that you are about to embark on will not be an easy walk, but remember, the race is not given to the swift but to those who endure to the end.

Be blessed with heaven's best. I love you!

About the Author

Dr. Cassundra White-Elliott resides in California with her family, where as an English/Education professor, she teaches at various community colleges.

When writing, she composes with the direction of the Holy Spirit, in an effort to share with God's people all He has for them.

In addition to teaching and writing, Dr. Elliott also serves as an evangelistic teacher. She is also the founder of International Women's Commission, a ministry that serves the needs of the entire person, by attending to healing the mind, body, soul, and spirit.

Dr. Elliott holds a Ph.D. in Education, a Master's degree in English Composition, and a Bachelor's degree in Education.

Dr. Elliott is the founder and editor-in-chief for *Christian Inspiration* magazine, which covers topics germane to Christian living and the world at large.

Dr. Elliott is also the founder of CLF Publishing, LLC. For your publishing needs, go online to www.clfpublishing.org.

www.ingramcontent.com/pod-product-compliance
Lightning Source LLC
LaVergne TN
LVHW021713080426
835510LV00010B/979